THE 7:56 REPORT
John Clarke

THE 7·56 REPORT

John Clarke

Text Publishing
Melbourne Australia

The Text Publishing Company
Swann House
22 William St
Melbourne Victoria 3000
Australia
www.textpublishing.com.au

This edition published 2006

Printed and bound by Griffin Press
Page design by Chong Weng-ho
Typeset in Stempel Garamond by J & M Typesetting

National Library of Australia
Cataloguing-in-Publication data:

Clarke, John, 1948- .
The 7.56 report : an official inquiry into just about
everything.
ISBN 9781921145698.
ISBN 1 921145 69 2.

1. 7.30 report (Television program). 2. Political satire,
Australian. 3. Politicians - Australia - Caricatures and
cartoons. 4. Australia - Politics and government - Humor.
I. Title.

320.9940207

This book is dedicated to
Bryan Dawe.
An ornament to the game.
Thanks for joining me.

CONTENTS

A NOTE ON THE CHARACTERS IN AUSTRALIAN PUBLIC LIFE

As Mr Dickens and Mr Thackeray have established in earlier works in this series, names are often a useful guide to the understanding of character. Think of Mr Pumblechook, the odious Uriah Heep, Mr Dobbin and the marvellous Mr Magwitch, (part magic, part witch) late of New South Wales.

Between these covers we are introduced to Mr Howard, whose name is not quite 'hero' and not quite 'coward', and who took his current position from the appropriately depressing Mr Downer and the unfortunate Mr Peacock. We also meet the somewhat green Mr Bush, the slightly frayed Mr Warne and the open and very welcoming Mr Dawe.

For those who may have just joined us, the following characters also crop up from time time, as the story requires:

Mr Costello.	A combination of cost and hello. A man who diminishes wealth cheerily.
Mr Vaile.	One who deals in secrets. Possibly in trade.
Mr Ruddock.	A combination of rodent and buttock. Not a happy fellow. Doomed.
Amanda Vanstone.	Amanda, a fixer. Van stone, up front and hard.
Mr Abetz.	One who helps. Not the one who has the actual idea.
Mr Minchin.	A pinched person; one who munches at society's vitals.
Mr Abbott.	One who does the work of some sort of religious order.

Mrs Bishop. One who can move diagonally over any number of unoccupied squares.

Mr Latham. A combination of lathe and ham. A hand-crafted loose cannon.

Barnaby Joyce. Barter and choice conspiring to produce no result. Big hat. No cattle.

Mr Swan. One who drifts elegantly about on the surface of things.

Mr Turnbull. Forceful, larger than life; changeable, possibly given to rampage.

Mr Boswell. A big, genial, ruddy-faced character; part boss, part swell.

Mr Nelson. A man with a telescope to his famously blind eye. He sees no signal.

Mr Heffernan. Heifer, a young cow. Unpredictable. Absurd.

Mr Windschuttle. Imagines he is talking sense when he is simply shuttling the wind.

Mr Beazley. A swarming man who brings us out in hives.

GREAT EXPECTATIONS

2003

THE HON. RICHARD ALSTON, MINISTER FOR COMMUNICATIONS, INFORMATION TECHNOLOGY AND THE ARTS

In which the gamekeeper is caught poaching an egg

Senator Alston, thanks for your time.

Good evening, Bryan. Very nice to be on the program.

I wonder if I could have a word with you about the sale of Telstra.

Yes, indeed.

This has always appealed to you, hasn't it, the idea of selling Telstra?

Yes, frankly, it *has* always appealed to me.

Even when you said you weren't going to do it?

Well, we didn't say we weren't going to do it, Bryan. Be fair. We said we had no plans *at that time* to do it.

Yes. Why does it appeal to you so much?

I think it gives Australians an opportunity to invest in their own future, Bryan.

Australians already owned it, though, didn't they?

In the sense that they already owned it?

Yes, in that very narrow sense.

In that very limited sense, Bryan, yes, but they weren't deriving a benefit; they weren't actually getting a dividend, a return.

Minister, what about the people who bought into T2 at $7? They haven't done very well, have they?

I might say that when we do T3, there'll be first aid available at the Australian Stock Exchange.

Will there be bandaging?

Bandaging will be available. There will be triage in the foyer, obviously, Bryan, and there'll be an oxygen tent for anyone with a super fund.

Isn't there a fear that, if Telstra is going to be driven by the need to return a dividend to shareholders, the less profitable services are going to be cut?

That will be up to the shareholders.

Yes, but isn't that the point? You're the minister who's responsible for delivering these services and they're not being…

We are delivering the services. Services have improved out of sight, especially in the bush.

You're satisfied that these services…?

Bryan, we've gone right through the thirty-nine points and we have improved things out of sight.

But, Minister, how do you measure that? Why are so many people out there still clearly unhappy?

We've got various ways of measuring it. You can measure it by simply making a phone call. *(He dials a number.)* I'll show you. Services in the bush are hugely improved. *(He speaks into the phone.)* I'd like a number in Queensland, please.

AUTOMATED RESPONSE: *Answering yes or no, is 'Buying off the National Party' correct?*

No, no. I won't keep you a minute, Bryan. *(Into phone.)* I'd like to speak to somebody about Telstra services in the bush, please.

AUTOMATED RESPONSE: *Answering yes or no, is 'We think Senator Boswell's on board' correct?*

(Into phone.) Can I speak to your supervisor, please? I want to know about bush services.

AUTOMATED RESPONSE: *Answering yes or no, is 'Why don't you just make the phone system work properly' correct?*

(Into phone.) Get me a bloody human being. I don't want to talk to a computer.

AUTOMATED RESPONSE: *Answering yes or no, is 'All the brokers think this is a turkey' correct?*

(To Bryan.) There are a couple of wrinkles that just need ironing out but the services are greatly improved. *(Into phone.)* No, that is incorrect, you clown!

AUTOMATED RESPONSE: *I'm afraid I didn't hear you.*

(Into phone.) I want to talk to somebody about services in the bloody bush.

AUTOMATED RESPONSE: *Answering yes or no, is 'I wouldn't worry about it, it'll never get through the Senate' correct?*

(Into phone.) No, it is not correct, you clown.

Senator Alston, thank you very much for coming in.

Just thank yourself for coming in, Bryan. I'm a bit busy.

Thank you, Bryan, for coming in.

AUTOMATED RESPONSE: *Answering yes or no, is 'Where are the weapons of mass destruction' correct?*

(Into phone.) No, you idiot!

THE HON. JOHN HOWARD, PRIME MINISTER OF AUSTRALIA

In which Bryan stumbles upon a great truth

Mr Howard, thanks for your time.

Good to see you, Bryan. Very good to be on the program.

I wanted to ask you a few things *very* quickly.

Yes, by all means. Certainly.

Obviously you're not going to be available next week.

Pardon? Why wouldn't I be available next week Bryan? I think I should be available next week.

Well, not unless they get the dispute sorted out. So, I just want to get a couple of very quick responses from you…

What dispute is this, Bryan?

I'll just throw a couple of questions and if you could just give me some quick responses.

I don't understand. What's the dispute that will keep me unavailable next week?

You've got the actors' dispute looming, Mr Howard, so I will just chuck you a few questions…

Actors' dispute? I don't understand quite how an actors' dispute would make *me* unavailable next week. What's the…

Well, if you don't sort it out, you're going to be on strike next week.

But how will an actors' strike affect me, Bryan? I'm not an actor.

Mr Howard, of course you're an actor. I've seen you on television.

Of course I'm on television, Bryan. I'm the prime minister of the country.

Yes, and I think you're really good. I think you are the best thing in the series to be perfectly honest.

I don't know what you're talking about, Bryan. I have absolutely no idea what you're talking about.

Oh, Mr Howard, come on. OK, Mr Howard, if you're not in the country, who takes your job?

The acting prime minister would do the job.

The *acting* prime minister. Exactly. There you go.

Bryan. I am not…

Hang on. Are you a member of Actors' Equity?

Of course not. Why would I be a member of Actors' Equity?

They'll be after you. They don't like that; working without being paid up.

Why would I be a member of Actors' Equity, Bryan? I'm not an actor.

You're not an actor? But your stand-in is? If you're unavailable your understudy acts in your position? Come on, please, Mr Howard…

I'm not an actor, I assure you.

That's fine. You take that view if you wish. It doesn't matter what you call yourself.

It does matter what I call myself, Bryan—I am called the prime minister! I call myself that and so does everyone else.

And as I said, you're very, very good. I see you on television every week. You're terrific.

Of course I'm on television! Bryan, I'm on television every week in connection with my *work*.

Mr Howard, actors are on television in connection with their work all the time. All the time, all of them. Don't be silly.

Bryan, what have you ever seen me in?

I saw you in *WMDs*. I thought you were fantastic. I thought the script was awful, but you were terrific.

I didn't write that script, actually.

I know, and didn't it show. But you were really, really good. I saw you in *The Defence of David Hicks*.

I didn't write that script either, I might say.

No, again, the script was awful, but you were really fantastic. How do you remember your lines?

It wasn't easy in that case. Did you see, *Peter Gives up Altogether and Buggers Off*?

I did. Loved it to bits.

Because I did write that.

Did you write that?

Yes.

I thought you were both fabulous in that.

What were your other questions, Bryan, just quickly?

You know what they are. You probably got the script before I did.

OK, we'll cut there thank you. Can somebody ring George Bush?

There are holes in this *Roadkill for Peace* script you could drive a truck through.

Hang on, Mr Howard. Isn't it *Roadmap for Peace*?

Oh dear. We've got two problems…get him fast, will you?

Thanks for your time.

That'll be the dinner break, Bryan. They'll need to shift the lights.

THE HON. MARK LATHAM, LEADER OF THE OPPOSITION

In which the contender spars with the press

Mr Latham, thanks for coming in.

Pleasure.

How are you?

Good thanks.

How are you enjoying the new job?

Not bad. Not bad. Growing into it.

Because you weren't very happy with your old position, were you?

I felt a bit restricted there.

Yes, you can get stuck, can't you?

Well, yes. And one thing I've learned in life is that you have to create your own opportunities.

And how do you do that?

It's not easy.

How did *you* do it?

I had to back over a bloke.

And the new job would be pretty demanding, wouldn't it?

It can be, but a great challenge.

The hours would be a lot longer, wouldn't they?

No. The hours themselves aren't any longer.

No, I don't mean the hours themselves.

You mean the number of hours?

Yes.

Yes. The workload is bigger.

Any problems?

One. I was cleaning my foreign policy the other night.

And it went off?

Actually, I shouldn't say it's mine. I share it with another bloke.

Who's this?

Kevin someone. Little bloke. Queensland.

You're job-sharing?
It's my responsibility. It's just that it's his responsibility too.
So you're not doing half the job each?
No, we're both doing all of it.
How does that actually work?
Yes, that's where we're taking a bit of water. It'd work if he didn't keep fiddling with the settings on the dials.
Isn't it his job?
It is, but I'm his boss.
Can you give me an example?
Sure. Have you got one of those little jars?
Not a sample. An example. How has this difference over foreign affairs been a problem?
Take the government's foreign policy.
The alliance with the US.
Yes. 'Do as you're told, no matter how moronic it is.' We're opposed to that.
Yes, and you've said so?
Yes, and my popularity went up.
And then what happened?
I kept going. I said we were going to bring everyone home for Christmas.
And what happened?
My popularity went down.
Why?
And the other bloke…
Kevin someone.
Yes, little bloke.
From Queensland.
Yes. He changes his policy from 'Hang on a minute we've only got one alliance. Don't poop in the nest.'
And what was his new policy?
He just followed me around wearing a hat with 'I'm with Stupid' written on it.

Didn't you want him to stop fiddling with the dials?

I did, but if we both play dumb people might forget how clever we are.

And how clever *are* you?

Individually I think we're very clever.

What about together?

Yes, there's your trouble.

THE HON. ALEXANDER DOWNER, MINISTER FOR FOREIGN AFFAIRS

In which the law is heard braying very loudly

Alexander Downer, thanks for your time.
It's a great pleasure, Bryan, and good evening.
Can you explain the position of David Hicks to us, please?
Yes, indeed. The David Hicks case is one I'm very familiar with.
He's an Australian citizen arrested by the Americans in Afghanistan.
He is, yes.
And what has he been charged with?
He hasn't been charged with anything yet, Bryan. But I'd say he's obviously guilty.
Guilty of what, Mr Downer?
Yes, good point. He hasn't been charged so he can't be guilty of…
How long has he been in jail, Mr Downer?
He's been incarcerated for, I think, about nineteen months.
In Cuba?
In the Caribbean, Bryan, yes. Have you ever been up there?
No, I haven't.
It's a lovely spot, the Caribbean. It's an absolute cracker. If you're ever given the opportunity, I'd whistle up there quick-smart.
I'll make a note of that. Mr Downer, has David Hicks seen a lawyer?
I doubt that he would have seen a defence lawyer.
But he would have seen a prosecuting lawyer?
He may have seen one or two prosecution lawyers, yes.
A Cuban?
I would think an American in his case.
Mr Downer, is that fair?
From what I understand, Bryan, he's lucky to see any bloody lawyer at all. He was training with al-Qa'ida. He was training in the use of weapons with al-Qa'ida.
Mr Downer, who told you that?

The Americans, Bryan. I'm not a fool. I've spoken to the prosecutors.

But he hasn't been tried yet, has he? How long is he going to be there? That is my point.

He's obviously guilty, Bryan.

You keep saying this, but guilty of what?

I don't know what he's being charged with, Bryan, but what I'm indicating to you is he probably bloody did it.

(Sighs.) **Mr Downer, are you familiar with the trial of Roger Casement?**

Roger Casement?

No? Doesn't ring a bell?

It's not an Adelaide name, Bryan, no.

Roger Casement was a citizen of one country, he was kidnapped in that country, taken to another country and then tried for treason in that second country.

He was taken from one country, removed to another country and tried for treason in respect of that second country, which wasn't the country he came from?

Correct. And then executed.

Executed! Good Lord.

Do you see any similarities?

Yes, I do.

Like what?

Guilty as buggery, the pair of them, Bryan.

A RELIGIOUS LEADER

In which we are asked to turn to our song sheets and sing Psalm 23 backwards

Thanks for your time.
Good evening. Very nice of you to invite me on the program, and good evening.
There seems to be a crisis in the Church, doesn't there?
There is, in fact, yes, a debate in the Church at the moment.
What exactly is going on?
There is a body of opinion in the Church that the Church has perhaps too many members.
But aren't church numbers in decline?
Yes. I think the feeling of this group, however, is that they could be in faster decline; that they are perhaps not declining with sufficient rapidity.
How would you achieve this?
There is a plan in place already and it has begun to rid the Church of certain groups altogether.
Yes. They want to get rid of gay people, don't they?
Actually, I think they're hoping to do better than that.
In what way?
Well, they will get rid of a lot of gay people. And they will clearly, by definition, get rid of a lot of other people in the Church community who are opposed to discrimination. And they will also get rid of a lot of other people who think the Church should be an inclusive body.
A bit like Christianity.
A little bit along the lines, Bryan, of a Christian church.
Why do you think the prime minister needed to enter this debate this week?
I think the prime minister was attempting to make a contribution. I think he thought he could make a contribution to the debate.
He said that gay people don't do anything to ensure the survival of the species.

Yes. It was unfortunate what he said, Bryan, but I think he was trying to help…

Survival of the species is not a function of sexual orientation.

As you say. I think it was unfortunate what the prime minister said. My point is I think he was trying to contribute.

Do you think what he was really trying to say was that gay people can't have children?

I don't know what he was trying to say.

Plenty of gay people have had children since the beginning of time, haven't they?

Yes, of course, gay people have had children forever. In fact, I've sent him a couple of brochures, which I hope he gets time to read. I think they're very helpful. They're relatively simple.

They have some diagrams in them?

They're quite graphic in some instances, Bryan, and very clear on the issue of eggs, and all that palaver, yes.

What does he say about heterosexuals who can't have children?

I've no idea what he says, Bryan. My point is I think he was trying to contribute to the debate and I think he was doing it very sincerely.

Does he think he's helping to solve the crisis in the Church?

Oh, I don't think anybody could imagine they were helping to do that by saying the things he said. But I think he's very sincere.

He may be sincere, but who is he trying to help?

I've no idea who he's trying to help. My point is he's doing it very sincerely, Bryan.

When's the next election?

I don't know. I don't think he's announced that yet.

Thanks for coming in.

It's a pleasure. What are you doing Sunday? We need the numbers.

Oh, I'm sorry, I'm busy Sunday.

Can you sing?

Yes.

What are you doing Sunday?

Singing.

THE HON. PHILIP RUDDOCK, ATTORNEY GENERAL

In which our hearts swell with pride

Mr Ruddock, thanks for joining us.

Good evening. It's very good to be with you.

I see in the paper that you've been in Parliament for almost thirty years?

Yes, that's right. Obviously, I've been home a couple of times in the interim, Bryan, but, broadly speaking, yes.

There have been a few anniversaries just recently, haven't there? It's been about two years since the Norwegian ship the *Tampa*...

Yes, that's right. That's an interesting coincidence. Quite true, Bryan.

Australia's position on this was widely criticised, wasn't it?

Only internationally, Bryan.

No, there's been criticism inside Australia as well, hasn't there?

Well, again, only on matters of substance.

And morally.

I beg your pardon?

And morally.

No, you're dropping out. I'm not getting your question there, Bryan.

Can we discuss this difficulty you've got with the court judgment the other day?

Yes, this is the one in the Family Court?

Yes.

Look, Bryan, the thing you've got to understand about judges—and let me be very clear about this—they're not elected at all.

That's right. This is the separation of powers, isn't it?

My point is that judges are spared more or less entirely the business of going about the place and saying things to people that they think will fool people into voting for them.

That's right. They're dealing with the law.

They have absolutely no idea about the process of government whatsoever.

No, Mr Ruddock. They do understand the role of government. In fact, in this case they're saying what the government did was illegal.

We'll be appealing.

Really? Are you sure?

I'm absolutely positive.

When do you think you'll be appealing?

We'll be talking to our legal people about when and where we do it.

I see, I beg your pardon. I'm sorry. I misunderstood what you meant by 'appealing'.

I expect to win that appeal too, Bryan.

Mr Ruddock, how do you feel when you see the first of the *Tampa* refugees being granted asylum in Australia and beginning to settle in?

(Off.) Can I have a glass of water, please?

Can we get Mr Ruddock a glass of water? Have you spoken to Mr Howard about this?

(Off.) Just a glass of water, thanks.

You must be very pleased. You've managed to process a whole twenty-four refugees in two years. That would be a world record, wouldn't it, Mr Ruddock?

(Off.) It doesn't matter about the size of the glass. I'm just a bit dry in the throat.

(Off.) **I don't think he's taking any notice.**

(Off.) Just a simple glass of water.

I think we'd better leave it there. I don't think we can continue with the interview, Mr Ruddock.

Are we finished?

Yes.

(Off.) And a glass of champagne, please—have you got a jeroboam?

THE HON. BOB McMULLAN, MEMBER FOR FRASER

In which gums are snatched from the jaws of defeat

Mr McMullan, thanks for your time.
It's very good to be here, Bryan. And thank you very much for inviting me on the program.

You've dropped your opposition to the GST.
The ALP has dropped its opposition to the GST, yes. We've put that behind us. It's a dark period. We've lost that one. It's time we moved on.

No more rollback?
No more rollback. Rollback's gone.

Incidentally, what was rollback?
I've got no idea, Bryan. We couldn't work it out.

Neither could we.
We had no idea in the party room. I imagine something was going to be rolled back, but I don't know what, or how.

So now we've got 'roll over'.
No. That's incorrect, Bryan. We're not rolling over. I suppose the best way to express this…

Rolling forward.
We're rolling forward, if you want to keep with the roll analogy. We're in a new policy environment, put it that way.

So basically you've given up.
No, we haven't given up, Bryan. We haven't given up at all. But there comes a point beyond which it's pointless to deal with the world as you would wish it to be. We need to deal with the world as it is. Are you familiar with the story of King Canute, for example?

No, what was the Canute story?
I've got no idea, I was rather hoping you would remember it.

No, no idea I'm afraid. So what is your policy with regard to the GST now?

Our policy is, in effect, as you say, roll forward. We want to make sure that the monies are gathered appropriately and that the allocations are fair and reasonable and the money is spent on things we genuinely need.

What is it spent on now?

We think it's spent pretty well.

And who spends it?

It is currently spent by the states, Bryan.

The states are run by Labor governments.

They are indeed, yes.

So you wouldn't have a problem with that?

No. They're going very, very well. They're doing an excellent job.

Although they haven't reduced stamp duties or other taxes of that type.

No, they haven't had time as yet, Bryan.

Do you think they will?

No I don't. But they certainly haven't had time as yet.

That's just an excuse.

And a very good one it is, too, Bryan. The point is that the other tax monies go directly to the federal government. It's not all given to the states.

Oh, this is the income tax…

Income taxes, company taxes. All the other direct and indirect taxes.

And what are they spent on?

As I understand it at the moment, Bryan, they're going on razor wire and American foreign policy.

You wouldn't be opposed to that.

We're devoutly opposed to that, Bryan.

No, you're not. You didn't oppose the government on the asylum seekers. And you certainly didn't oppose going to the war in Iraq.

Not at the time, Bryan, no. But we are devoutly opposed to those things now. We're the opposition in this country…

Of course.

And look at the trouble we're in.

Australia or the Labor Party?

Australia. We are now living through one of the great international policy failures of the last fifty years.

Mr McMullan, have you got anything left that you were opposed to at the time?

Something we were opposed to at the time, publicly, and which we are still opposed to?

Yes. Something we can make sense of.

As a party? Something we've been consistent on, yes. Over what period?

A year.

A year! Good heavens. I'd be surprised if we've got the same policies on Monday.

Mr McMullan, thanks for your time.

(*Off. Astonished.*) Did you hear the question, Dave?

THE HON. MARK LATHAM, LEADER OF THE OPPOSITION

In which we share quality time with Mary Shelley

Mr Latham, thanks for your time.

It's very good to be here, Bryan. Thanks for the invitation.

Congratulations, by the way.

Thank you, thank you. It's a great honour for me personally, and a healing time for the party. We move now into the future; into a broad, sunlit upland. *(Bryan is donning protective clothing.)* What are you doing, Bryan?

I'm just getting ready.

Getting ready for what? I don't understand.

I'm going to interview you.

I realise you're going to interview me, Bryan. But what is all this stuff? I'm not fully aware of what you're doing there.

This is a protective helmet and some slightly more resilient, industrial clothing.

To protect you against what?

I've got a couple of questions I want to ask you about the government.

But I don't understand. What's this thing here?

This is just a large bit of plastic. It covers up my suit.

Covers your suit? What are you trying to protect yourself from?

In case I ask you a couple of questions about the US.

You haven't asked any questions at all yet, Bryan.

No, I'm not quite ready. I just want to make sure I'm fully kitted up—

I don't know where the interview is going.

I'm nearly ready.

I think you can over-prepare.

I just want to make certain we're ready, that's all.

A box? What do you need a box for?

I'm going to ask you some questions, maybe, that involve the PM.

And the last time I did that…

What happened?

It took a week and a half to clean out the studio.

Well, look, Bryan. If I could say to you and to the broader Australian public, you're not going to need that. That's just silly.

So you've reformed?

I have reformed. I am a completely different person now, Bryan. I've stopped that altogether.

So who are you now?

I'm still Mark Latham, Bryan, but I have a completely different set of personal standards as regards my behaviour.

(Bryan pulls on protective welding goggles.) **I won't be long.**

You'll be perfectly safe, don't have any anxiety about—

OK. Are you ready?

For the interview? I've been ready for the interview for some time.

(Bryan hides behind his chair, peeping out.) Where are you going?

Just here.

We're about to do the interview?

Certainly. Are you right?

Yes, indeed.

Mr Latham, what do you think of John Howard aligning Australia with the US?

(The building explodes and a firestorm consumes the area.)

OUR MUTUAL FRIEND

2004

MR ZIGGY SWITKOWSKI, A SERVICE PROVIDER

In which we glimpse real leadership

Ziggy Switkowski, thanks for your time.

Pleasure.

(A mobile phone is ringing.) **Is that yours or mine?**

Sorry, that's mine.

It's best to turn it off in here.

OK, how long will we be?

We won't be long. Couple of minutes. Can't they text you?

Good point. I'll flick it over. Have you got a pair of binoculars?

Why?

The buttons on these things are so small. I can never read them.

Yes, they're tiny aren't they? I'm always dialling wrong numbers.

Yes, there are some advantages but it's nevertheless very annoying.

We won't be long.

It's just that if something crops up at a moment's notice I need to be contactable.

Of course. What sort of thing might crop up?

There's a 'Bring and Buy' up in Cooma tonight. They might just have to ring me if there's something good there.

Something good?

Yes, there are some good things at some of these sales.

What sort of things?

Stoves. Wooden tennis racquets.

Why are you looking for things to buy?

I run Australia's biggest telephone company.

This is Telstra?

Yes.

Of course.

And we've got a lot of money. What's that thing?

That's a camera.

What do you want for it?

It's not for sale. It belongs to the ABC.

What would it be worth?

Fifty thousand.

I'll give you a hundred thousand.

That's double what it's worth.

See! You're thinking about it now.

Mr Switkowski, what do your shareholders think of all this?

All what?

Well, wouldn't they like some money returned to them as a dividend?

This isn't coming out of the dividend fund.

What's it coming out of?

It's coming out of the fund for buying old stuff out of people's sheds.

Would you be interested in a bike?

What sort of bike?

It's a Malvern Star.

Yes. What year. Has it got turbo?

No, it's a bike.

Great what's it worth?

Twenty bucks.

I'll give you a hundred. Hang on, two hundred. Make it three hundred.

MESSRS KEELTY, HILL AND LATHAM

In which the English language hums like a top

OK. Now, I'll get to all of you as fast as possible. First, Mick Keelty, thanks for your time.

Pleasure.

You've got a clarification you'd like to make?

Yes, look, thanks for giving me the opportunity. I may have misled people the other day with this statement I made.

This is the one about national security?

Yes.

In your capacity as commissioner of the Federal Police?

That's right.

And what was the difficulty?

Just that the prime minister and I had a different way of expressing things maybe.

Different word use.

No I don't think either of us used the word 'different'.

What was it that you had said?

I advanced the view that the likelihood of Australia being a terrorist target had increased by our involvement in the War on Iraq.

Yes. And what would you like to say now?

I'd like to say that the likelihood of Australia being a terrorist target had increased by our involvement in the Mittagong Begonia Festival.

The Mittagong Begonia Festival?

Yes, I think that's what it says.

Who is Arthur Sinodinos?

He's the prime minister's begonia bloke.

A begonia expert?

Yes.

How would that cause an increased risk to national security?

You can't be too careful, Bryan.

I'll be all right. I've got a fridge magnet. Robert Hill, you've got a correction to make as well, haven't you?

Yes, thanks Bryan.

You're the Minister for Defence.

Yes that's right. Australian Federal Minister for Defence.

And what is your correction?

I said during the week that there are no weapons of mass destruction in Iraq.

And what did you mean?

I meant that there were no weapons of mass destruction in 'Irene Goodnight'.

In 'Irene Goodnight'. In the song 'Irene Goodnight'.

Yes.

No weapons of mass destruction in the song?

None at all.

Well you should know, you're the Minister for Defence. Mr Latham, you've got something you wish to correct?

Yes. Gidday, Bryan.

What is it you wish to correct?

I made a statement in the Parliament the other day.

Oh yes. What statement was this?

It was about Alexander Downer.

OK, what did you say about Alexander Downer?

I called him a rotten, lousy rotten disgrace.

And you've had time to think about that now, have you?

Yes, I deeply regret that statement. That was inappropriate.

And what do you want to say now?

Alexander Downer is a snobby dickhead from Adelaide.

A different sort of disgrace?

Yes. I shouldn't have said it. I'm sorry, Alexander.

THE HON. JOHN HOWARD, PRIME MINISTER OF AUSTRALIA

In which the prime minister makes no attempt to hide his passion for whatever

Mr Howard, thanks for your time.
Pleasure.
You've announced a $365 million early childhood package.
Yes I have, Bryan. A very important initiative of great benefit to
Australian families.
Yes. What is it?
Works out at a million dollars a day. Three hundred and sixty-five
days, 365 million.
Yes. How does it work?
Yes, hang on. I've got this written down somewhere.
The opposition has dismissed this as a pre-election bribe.
They would, wouldn't they.
Why?
Because we announced it in response to their pre-election bribe they
announced the other day.
So theirs is a pre-election bribe but yours isn't?
Here you go. 'This is based on the twin concepts of social cohesion and
early intervention.'
What does that mean?
That means those are the two central elements in the plan.
Social cohesion and early intervention?
That's right. Cohesion. 'Co' meaning 'with'; co-venture, co-operate,
co-mbine.
Combine?
Yes. To join something with something else.
Cohesion?
With hesion.
With hesion?
Yes.

There hasn't been enough hesion?

There has been insufficient hesion, Bryan, in early childhood for some time.

And early intervention. What does that mean?

That means not intervening too late. There's no point in intervening too late. If you're going to intervene too late you might ask yourself whether it's worth intervening at all.

In what?

In anything. This is the thing about intervention.

If you're going to do it, do it early.

That's the key point.

Yes, but why intervene at all?

In early childhood?

Yes.

We believe it's the best way to get in there and make sure there's enough hesion.

What exactly *is* hesion?

I don't know. This would all be done by experts.

Hesion experts?

Hesionologists will be airlifted in, Bryan, into those areas of early childhood.

Where the hesion has been lacking?

Where there has hitherto been a paucity, yes, of hesion.

Mr Howard, can free trade be explained like this?

There are some problems with logic and free trade.

Why?

Because it's not free and there are certain respects in which it's not trade and we're not entirely sure it's going to happen at all.

What about aged care?

Look, I'll be right. I've got parliamentary super.

Thanks for your time.

Precisely.

THE HON. JOHN HOWARD, PRIME MINISTER OF AUSTRALIA

In which we hold sacred the things we have not done

Mr Howard, thanks for your time.
Pleasure.
You haven't had much of a week have you?
People keep telling me things that aren't true.
Do you check what you're being told?
Yes.
When?
About a year later.
Tell us about this business of going to the D-day celebrations.
Yes, well I've got a long association with the Anzac tradition of course.
Yes.
My grandfather was in the First World War.
Yes. Do we have any figures on this sort of thing in Australia?
On what sort of thing?
The number of people in Australia who are descended from people who had children?
The point is my grandfather fought in the war.
Yes, I know that.
How did you know that?
Someone must have broken into your house and stolen some photographs of him.
Really.
Yes. I saw them in the paper.
In uniform?
Yes. In France in the First World War.
Good heavens!
They must have been stolen from your own private collection. How else would the newspaper have got hold of the photos?
Yes.

For the fourth year in a row.

Yes. Is it just at that time of the year?

Just in that weekend before Anzac Day, yes.

Every year.

Yes.

Yes there's a pattern there, isn't there?

You do a bit of this don't you. You went to Baghdad.

Yes I did. We got some of the most senior journalists in the country in and we told them I was going.

Yes. I was there.

Yes of course you were, and we told them not to tell anyone.

Yes. Why did you tell us not to tell anyone?

Because of the security risk. If anyone knew I was going, there could have been a security risk.

So why tell us?

Because we didn't want anyone to know.

Why not just go? Why tell us and then tell us not to tell anyone?

We only told the most senior journalists. We didn't tell just anyone not to tell anyone.

Yes, but why tell anyone at all? If not telling people was the purpose, why tell us and tell us not to tell people?

If you want people not to know what's going on, you've got to speak to people who are experts.

In keeping information from the general public.

In acting in the national interest, in this case.

You tell the senior-most political journalists.

That's what we decided to do.

Now people want to know what else we're not telling them.

Don't tell them, will you?

Don't tell them what?

That's right. That's very good. So look, we were here, the photo opportunity was over here. We had to get around the back of here with only a camera crew and a fully basted turkey.

Did you have covering fire?

Yes.

Who from?

From you. We've covered that.

Thank you.

Thank *you*, Bryan.

THE HON. JOHN HOWARD, PRIME MINISTER OF AUSTRALIA

In which a great problem gets a fifty-year start on police

Mr Howard, thanks for your time.

Pleasure.

Would you mind just explaining to me the government's policy on renewable energy.

Certainly. The government of Australia?

Yes.

Yes. Government's policy on what?

On renewable energy.

We're in favour of it.

I think everyone's in favour of it.

Yes, it's renewable.

That's right. You use it and it's there again.

Yes, unlike non-renewable sources of energy.

Which are gone.

You use them and they're gone.

So what is the government's policy on this issue?

Obviously the government's policy on this issue is to favour in terms of allocating research resources and funding, the renewable forms of energy, Bryan, the ones that don't damage the air and the earth and the sea.

You're reading that upside down.

I beg your pardon. The government favours the fossil fuel forms of energy, Bryan, the ones that damage the air and the earth and the sea.

Why would that be, Mr Howard?

There are fossil fuels.

Coal, oil and gas.

Exactly. And 90 per cent of our energy needs are provided from those fossil fuels.

From burning fossil fuels?

Yes, therefore we don't need to develop renewable ones.

Isn't that a powerful reason why we *do* have to develop new clean forms of energy?

We can't.

Why not?

There's solar power, wind power and wave power.

That's right. We're in a great position to develop all of them.

Bryan, solar power is from the sun. Australia doesn't have enough sunlight to do that.

Australia's one of the sunniest places on earth.

Not at night.

What about wind power?

Again, no wind.

We're the biggest island in the world. There's wind all the time.

Yes, but how do you get it? You can't just reach up and grab some wind.

Wind turbines.

Dangerous.

How?

They make noise.

They're working on that.

We'll stop them.

What about wave power?

No waves.

We're surrounded by the sea.

Except from the sea.

Mr Howard, *(There is a flash.)* **thanks for your time.**

Why did the light go on?

Wind power.

THE HON. PETER COSTELLO, TREASURER OF AUSTRALIA

In which an important government marketing plan walks and chews gum at the same time

Mr Costello, thanks for your time.

That's a great family, Bryan, and thanks for the invitation. Good to have a bit of a family with you.

Pardon?

It's good to see you, Bryan. Good to be here.

Mr Costello, this is your ninth budget.

Yes, it's a family budget.

You've got a big surplus.

Yes, the important family was working out what to do with it.

That was the important question.

Family is always an important question, Bryan.

I'm interested in a couple of things you've done here with the surplus.

You've got a family haven't you?

Have I got a family?

Yes.

Yes.

Yes, have they got families?

Has my family got families?

Yes, your family must have a family or they wouldn't be a family.

I suppose my family has a family, yes.

Very important, Bryan. There's nothing more important in Australia, in our way of life, than voting.

Than family.

There's nothing more family in our way of voting, than Australia.

Mr Costello, are you trying to become the prime minister, or the editor of the *Good Weekend*?

No, I'm the treasurer, Bryan. I'm very happy being the treasurer.

Every now and again we get these same stories about Mr Howard

standing aside for you to take over the leadership of the party.

Yes. Don't know where they come from, Bryan.

They're an accident.

Nobody could have been more surprised than I was to see all this come up again just when I was about to announce a huge surplus.

Are they different stories or the same one just run again and again?

From my reading it looked like the same story but with different photos.

You go out and shoot different photos?

Yes, we did.

Why?

I've got no idea, Bryan.

You don't know how it happens?

No idea.

You're very happy being the treasurer?

I'm delirious. I'm so happy I could do it for ever.

Mr Costello, if you were going to qualify for the $3000 for having a baby, and your doctor induced the birth a couple of days before the July 1 qualifying date, could you sue your doctor?

Not if the doctor had a family, Bryan.

So how does this all work, do you get the $3000 in the hospital?

No, you go out of the hospital, take your baby to any post office. It's franked, the parents are given some money to take to the casino and the infant is returned.

Isn't this going to take a lot of women out of the workforce?

Only if women are the ones having the babies.

Mr Costello, thanks for your time.

That's a great family, Bryan.

THE HON. ROBERT HILL, MINISTER FOR DEFENCE

In which a few simple precautions are seen to save a lot of trouble

Mr Hill, thanks for your time.

Pleasure. Are any of your questions about national security?

I don't know. What do you mean?

Are there any about the war? About all this business about the mistreatment of Iraqi prisoners?

Yes, a few.

Let's have a look.

Why?

Before we get going, there might be some here we might have to drop.

Why?

That one for example.

'If you use the media to spread propaganda, how can you be surprised when it turns around and bites you on the arse?'

Yes, that's a bit rude isn't it? The language.

We can change 'arse'. I can say 'bottom'.

No, 'propaganda'. We weren't using the media to spread propaganda.

What were you doing? You said they had weapons of mass destruction. You said we were restoring democracy. 'Propaganda' is cleaning it up a bit.

We were helping the media to understand the position, Bryan. And this will have to come out.

'Are you the Australian Defence Minister?'

Yes. And that one.

'Have you ever met Alexander Downer?'

And this.

'Does the name "John Howard" mean anything to you?'

Yes.

Why are these not appropriate questions?

And there's no point in asking me that one.

'Have you had a drink this evening, sir?'

I'll have a go at that one there.

That's not a question.

It could be phrased as a question.

Why do want it to be phrased as a question?

Because I know the answer.

But it just says the defence allocation has gone up in the budget.

Yes and I could say 'Yes it has, we're very committed to Australia's defence. We need to upgrade all our capabilities as a matter of urgency.' But I'm not answering that one there.

'Why do we need to upgrade all our defence capabilities as a matter of urgency?'

Yes. No going near that one. Here are a couple of good ones. I'll let you do those.

OK. Senator Hill, thanks for your time.

Pleasure.

How is the war going in Iraq?

No, not that one. The one below that.

Are you happy we got ourselves involved in this one?

Below that.

That's not a question to you. That's someone in our office writing that when I was preparing the interview.

Just read it, Bryan.

Would you like a cup of tea?

Love one thanks. Next one.

There are two here.

Let's have them both.

Milk?

Yes thanks.

Sugar?

No thanks, Bryan.

THE HON. MARK LATHAM, LEADER OF THE OPPOSITION

In which a keen boy brings something very special to show and tell

Mark Latham, thanks for your time.
Pleasure.

You've come in for some criticism this week over your backflip on pharmaceutical benefits.
Yes. It wasn't an easy decision.

Why was that?
Because if we got it wrong we were going to lose our traditional support base, older voters, the younger sort of socially conscious Green vote we'd been hoping to attract with Peter Garrett.

Political suicide?
Yes.

And how did you avoid that?
We didn't. That's what we did.

Commit political suicide?
We didn't have much choice.

Why not?
Well, if we hadn't done that we'd have maintained a lead.

So it's a pretty clever strategy.
It's brilliant.

Now that you've weakened your opposition to the Free Trade Agreement, what's the difference between the Labor Party and the government?
There is a difference.

What is it?
I've got it here.

Can we have a look?
Whoops!

Where is it?
On the floor. I've dropped it. Have you got a magnifying glass? Get a

magnifying glass will you?

How big was it?

It was about as big as an atom. Quite a big atom.

Would a magnet help?

No. It's not metallic. It's got to be somewhere.

What's that?

That's a speck of dust. We're looking for the difference between the government and the opposition. Maybe go to a break and we'll find it.

We don't do breaks. This is the ABC.

(Cuts back to Kerry O'Brien, who closes the show. Before the credits, cut back to Latham and Bryan. They are still searching the studio.)

Is this it?

No. That's a fly speck. It's not that big.

THE HON. ALEXANDER DOWNER, MINISTER FOR FOREIGN AFFAIRS

In which the history boys understand that they must get their story straight

Alexander, thanks for coming to see me.

That's OK.

Now, I've got your essay. I've just got a couple of questions.

Yes.

You say here that the terrorist threat to Australia has increased because of a decision made by the governments of Spain and the Philippines.

Yes.

What did you mean by that?

Just that…can I have a look at it?

Yes.

(*Reading.*) 'The terrorist threat to Australia has increased because of a decision made by the governments of Spain and the Philippines.' Yes.

OK, what did you mean, Alexander?

I meant that the threat of terrorism in Australia…

Yes.

Has gone up, because of action taken by the governments of Spain and the Philippines.

Yes. Have you got any reasoning here?

What do you mean 'reasoning'?

Have you got any footnotes? Is there anything in here to explain how this argument might work? I understand your contention. We've just got to see how you support it. What evidence have you got?

The threat of terrorism in Australia has gone up.

Yes, where does it say that? Where do you get your information from?

Another boy told me.

Who was he? Do you remember his name?

No. Spain and the Philippines have done things.

Yes, I'm sure a lot of countries have done things. The point is you're making a connection here. I want to see that connection.

Are all the pages there? Maybe not all the pages are there.

What do you mean?

Maybe a dog ate it.

I haven't got a dog.

I can lend you one.

I don't want to borrow a dog, Alexander. I'm trying to help you. This is pretty important. You've got some big exams coming up.

I'm allowed to say things.

But you've got to back them up. How would it be if the government carried on like this?

Just said stuff?

Yes.

They'd be allowed.

Alexander. Do you remember you wrote an essay on the cause of the war?

Yes, weapons of mass destruction.

Now you weren't quite right about that, were you?

No, but that's what one of the other kids told me.

Was that the same boy who told you the terrorist threat to Australia was linked to decisions by Spain and the Philippines?

Maybe.

Isn't it more likely that the terrorist threat to Australia will have something to do with actions by Australia?

Maybe.

You'll have to do it again, Alexander.

I'm not doing it again.

You'll fail. This doesn't make sense.

Doesn't have to.

Yes it does.

No it doesn't.

Why not?

My father owns the school.

HIS EXCELLENCY RICHARD BUTLER, CITIZEN

In which Little Red Riding Hood wonders why grandmother's cook has a chauffeur

Richard Butler, thanks for coming in.
Greetings.
This governor business has become rather unpleasant, hasn't it?
Yes, unfortunately, but I think we'll move on.
Can I ask you what is next for you?
Are there any better seats than these?
Better seats?
Yes. Can we be upgraded?
Upgraded?
Yes. We'll ask for an upgrade. Better view. The food's better too.
There's isn't any food.
Where's the pool? And let's get a bottle of something as well.
We don't do upgrades here.
You might not have done them to date, Bryan. Let's see. Where's the button?
What button?
The button for service.
There isn't a button.
How do you get service?
Mr Butler.
Lord Butler.
Lord Butler, we don't do service.
I'm a republican Lord.
Republican Lord Butler, we don't do service here. We're a broadcaster.
(He speaks into his lapel microphone.) Get me the manager will you?
Don't talk into that.
Hello. Republican Lord Butler here. Get me the manager please.
Don't do that.

And let's get some nibbles. We'll have a tray of larks' uvulas please to table. What table number is this?

Of what?

Of larks' uvulas. They're sautéed in yak's cheese. Beautiful.

Republican Lord Butler, the kitchen's closed.

Who runs the place?

It's owned by the government.

Public money.

That's right.

My favourite. We can open the throttle a bit. Have you got an elephant?

An elephant?

Yes, I always think an elephant's nice at one of these little occasions.

Republican Lord Butler, I don't think we can do this.

You don't want to do it any more?

I don't think we can. It's not working and we haven't got the budget.

You want to stop?

Yes.

Well that could run into money.

How much?

Have we got the larks' uvulas?

Can we get some larks' uvulas?

And an elephant. Each.

A SENIOR MILITARY GENTLEMAN

In which age wearies them and the years condemn

General, thanks for your time.
Pleasure. Stand easy. Gather round, lads.
I wonder if I can ask you about this letter you've signed about Australia's involvement in the Iraq war.
Yes, certainly.
You were a signatory?
Yes I was.
If we could just go to the government's criticisms of your argument.
Certainly.
How old are you?
I'm sixty-two.
Sixty-two.
Yes.
Righto. Next.
Pardon?
Send the next one, will you?
The next what?
There are more of you out there, aren't there? I've dealt with you.
You've dealt with me? How have you dealt with me?
You've criticised the government on going to war in Iraq?
That's right. I'm a general.
How old are you?
I'm sixty-two.
Thank you. Send in the next one, will you?
What's my age got to do with this?
You're not young.
I'm younger than the prime minister.
Yes, but he's still capable of holding a job down.
When we get to a certain age we have to retire.
Yes. A hint that was lost on you, wasn't it, pal.

It doesn't mean I don't know what I'm talking about. It doesn't mean I didn't go to two wars.

Isn't there some clown from the air force out there?

There's an air vice-marshal out there.

What's his job?

He's retired but he used to run the air force.

Used to. Right, well we don't have to bother with him. Is there a navy geriatric out there?

Does being retired mean you suddenly don't know anything?

Why aren't the current military criticising the government?

They'd be fired.

OK. So the air vice-marshal's area is aerial combat?

Yes.

Does he know as much about it as De-Anne Kelly?

Who's De-Anne Kelly?

Don't try and be clever. Does he know as much about it as De Anne-Kelly?

I've never heard of De-Anne Kelly.

Just answer the question. It's simple enough.

Does an air vice-marshal know as much about war and defence matters as De-Anne Kelly?

Yes. Let's phone a friend.

Whose friend are we dialling?

We're just dialling that number. Hello? Warren?

Yes.

Warren Entsch?

Yes. Who's that?

Bryan Dawe. We've got a question for you.

Hang on, I'll put my hat on.

Who would know more about Australia's defence and armed combat, an air vice-marshal or De-Anne Kelly?

Can we go for a 50/50?

It is a 50/50, Warren. Who would know more about defence and armed combat, an air vice-marshal or De-Anne Kelly?

How old is the air vice-marshal?

Younger than the prime minister.

De-Anne Kelly.

See? Send the next one in, will you?

A 'MASTERMIND' CONTESTANT

In which a contestant does surprisingly well

Your special subject is John Howard. Your time starts now. What will John Howard never bring in? Ever.

A GST.

Correct. When did John Howard bring in a GST?

The first of July, 2000.

Correct. What are weapons of mass destruction?

Sorry. Is that George on the phone?

Correct. If you know people want a republic, how do you get them to vote against it?

You ask them to vote for a republic where they don't get to vote for the President.

Correct. What is the Kyoto Agreement?

Something to do with coal prices?

Correct. What is the environment?

Pass.

Correct. What were being thrown overboard into the sea just before the last election?

Nothing.

I beg your pardon. I misread the question. What did John Howard *say* were being thrown overboard into the sea just before the last election?

The children of asylum seekers.

Correct. What did he do to prove it?

He released a film of it not happening.

Correct. Who told him the children *were* being thrown in the sea?

The Minister for Defence said he'd been told by the navy.

Correct. And what did the Minister for Defence do when the navy denied that?

He resigned and got a job selling defence contracts to the Australian government.

And was there a conflict there?

No. It was Peter Reith.

Correct. What about some of the other people in the Howard ministry. When they've retired, where have they retired to?

To jobs with companies who operate in the fields where they used to be the minister.

Correct. And would this have been worked out beforehand?

Shut your face.

Correct. What does the word 'integrity' mean?

Can you repeat the question?

Correct. If you make a promise and don't keep it, what was it?

A non-core promise.

Correct. Who can get married in Australia?

Marriage is between a man and a woman.

What if they don't like each other?

It doesn't matter if they hate each other's guts as long as one of them is a man and one of them is a woman.

Correct. Why don't we have to listen to senior members of the defence community criticise the government on defence?

They're too old.

Correct. Why don't we have to listen to ex public servants criticising the government's use of research information?

They're the scum of the earth, public servants.

Can you be more specific?

Get stuffed.

Correct. And at the end of that round your house is worth three times what you paid for it.

Great.

Congratulations.

Thanks. Three times what I paid for it!

Yes. Low interest rates. You're worth a fortune.

He's great, John Howard, isn't he?

He certainly is.

THE HON. PETER COSTELLO, TREASURER OF AUSTRALIA

In which the formalities are explained

Mr Costello, thanks for your time.

Pleasure.

Well at last we've got an election campaign.

Yes, we're up and running officially now. All the rituals have been enacted.

Yes, what are they?

Well I just mean the formalities. The prime minister goes to see the governor-general.

This is through the gate in the white car?

Yes with the three photographers there.

Yes, then what happens?

He informs the governor-general that there's to be an election. The governor-general announces the dissolution of both houses of Parliament…

Prorogues.

Prorogues, sorry, the Parliament. I announce that I'm not going to challenge John Howard for the leadership, then…

Yes, why do you always do that?

That's the way things have always been done.

But why do you have to point out that you're not going to challenge for the leadership?

Because people have got to know that if they vote for John Howard that's what they're going to get.

And now we're four or five days into the campaign, how do you think you're going?

We're going well.

Where have you been this week?

Various places.

What policies have you been pushing?

I've been concentrating on not issuing any kind of challenge to John Howard's leadership.

The prime minister has said the election is about trust.

That's right.

Doesn't the children overboard story militate against...

It's about trust on the big important issues. Trust in economic management.

Hasn't the huge deficit announced this week thrown that management into question?

It's about trust in those areas of economic management that don't bear particularly on the vagaries of monthly trade figures.

Why is the government so worried about the Greens?

Do you mean the attacks on the Greens in the newspapers?

Yes.

The government hasn't got anything to do with the newspapers.

Do you disagree with the newspapers?

To answer your earlier question, if people vote Green the Labor Party is going to get a lot of preferences and that could have a major effect on the outcome.

So how will you counter that?

What we're trying to do at the moment is let everyone know of the danger, without doing it too loudly.

Why don't you want to do it too loudly?

In case people do it.

Explain it again.

If people vote Green...

Why would they do that?

They don't trust the government and they don't like the opposition.

Sounds unlikely.

It's hypothetical.

Yes.

Their preferences could tip the government out?

Yes.

Shhhh...

(The janitor.) **Who's in there?**

(Both.) No one.

THE HON. JOHN ANDERSON,
DEPUTY PRIME MINISTER OF AUSTRALIA

In which man maketh the clothes

Mr Anderson, thanks for your time.
It's very good to be here, Bryan.

How do you think the campaign is going?
It's going very well.

It's an interesting campaign, isn't it?
It's extraordinarily interesting. We had the prime minister up the other day.

This is in the country clothing?
Yes, the tweed jacket.

And the flat hat?
Yes, and the moleskin strides.

Is he popular up there?
He's extraordinarily popular.

Will it be close, do you think, this election?
Yes, I don't think anyone's home yet.

What have been the highlights for you?
I've announced a lot of money for roads.

You do that a lot, don't you?
I do it whenever I can, Bryan. It's a great thing to do. Very satisfying.

Why do you get to do it?
We're the National Party. We're pretty interested in the bush and the rural and regional issues.

Which way did you vote on Telstra?
Telstra's going very well. Going very well in my area.

What area are you in?
I'm in the 1 per cent of the country where you can't get a signal.

And it's going well there, is it?
It's going extraordinarily well there.

So will you be making many other policy announcements

in the run-up to the election?

There may be some more roads funding announced.

There's not a lot you can announce, is there?

It's mostly roads, Bryan.

When do you announce more money for roads?

Whenever there's an election.

I imagine that's the time the announcements are most effective.

That's what we've found. People certainly seem to understand it better around election time.

Do you think they're *thinking* more about roads at that time?

That could be. They probably know they're going to have to go down a road to vote.

Didn't you *forget* to announce some money for roads once?

I did. It was a busy period.

You had a lot on.

I did. I think I was supposed to announce it but my notes were in my other trousers. And of course that money *did* go on roads.

It just didn't go on roads until later.

Yes.

Why is it this money's not spent on the roads the rest of the time?

A lot of it is. There are some repairs to roads all the time.

Yes, but 200 million. It's a lot.

That's right. It's a good point, Bryan. I'll ask about that.

Who will you ask?

I'll ask the prime minister.

Is he the Minister for Roads?

No, but he's in charge of the election. That's the time we get the money for roads.

Yes, well, that's my question.

I understand your question, Bryan.

Why is it only at election time?

I understand your question.

Will you be able to get an answer?

No, I don't think I will, but I understand it.

A VOTER, ELECTORATE OF UPPER SWING

In which we beard the problem in its lair

Thanks for coming in.

Good morning.

You're a voter?

Yes, I am.

In what electorate?

I'm in Upper Swing. That's the federal seat. We're in Hospitalfunding West in the state election.

No, I mean the federal seat. Upper Swing.

Yes. It's a redistribution, it's effectively a new seat.

Is Upper Swing a metropolitan electorate or is it rural?

Upper Swing is both. Do you know the area at all?

A bit, yes. I was through there the other day. It's near Floating isn't it?

It's between Floating and Undecided. Do you know where the Marketing Turnoff is?

Off the Blithering Highway?

Yes. Past Blithering. Do you know where you go past the foothills of the Whybotherings?

Yes. Near Drivel.

That's right. In behind Drivel.

Who's got the pub there now?

The 'Plough and Chequebook'?

Yes.

Roger Overndout.

So. Have you had the pollies up in Upper Swing lately?

Yes. We've had them all.

And what are they saying? They'd be running hard up there, wouldn't they?

The government's spending a billion dollars in the electorate.

Really? What on?

On a sign saying the government's spending a billion dollars in the electorate.

Are the opposition promising anything?

Yes, they're going to spend 2 billion.

What on?

They're going to take the government's sign down.

Yes?

And they are spending a billion and a half on education.

Education. That's a key issue at the moment. Where's the money being spent?

I don't know. There's an archbishop coming up to announce that on Sunday.

Are interest rates an issue for you up there?

Yes. Very much so. Seventeen per cent.

Hang on. Interest rates are low, aren't they? Hasn't Australia got low interest rates?

Every country's got low interest rates at the moment. But that's if you're borrowing to buy a house.

Yes, or a car or something.

Ten per cent if you're borrowing to buy a car.

Yes, but they're not 17 per cent.

I'm paying 17 per cent on my credit card.

Who told you that?

The doctor's wife told me that.

Yes. We're having a lot of trouble with doctors' wives at the moment. *(Dials phone.)* **Did she say anything about the war?**

The Iraq War. Yes, the American one. Yes, she doesn't understand what we're doing there.

Do you know her name?

Jennifer. She's very nice.

Surname?

Yes, good question. Hang on, she uses her own name

(Into phone.) **Hello. We've got another one.**

He's Dr Harrison. What is her name? *(Dials phone.)*

Not the same name as her husband?

No.

What's the point of having a wife if you can't control her? *(Into phone.)* **Hello. We've got another one. Jennifer someone.**

(Into phone.) I think we've got them worried.

(Into phone.) **I don't know. I'll ask. How many doctors are there in that area?**

She *said* you wouldn't know that. *(Into phone.)* No, they don't know.

THE HON. JOHN HOWARD AND MARK LATHAM

In which the property is now on the market

Mr Howard, thanks for coming in.

H: Pleasure.

Mr Latham, thanks for your time.

L: Pleasure.

H: Could I just get something understood, Bryan?

Mr Howard.

H: This is not a debate, is it?

No. This is not a debate. I just want to ask you some questions.

H: Good. I'm not covered for debates.

L: I'm not surprised.

What do you mean you're not covered?

H: It's an insurance issue. I'm not covered for debates. Small discussions I'm all right. It's just that if anything develops into a fully fledged debate, I'll have to pay for the damage myself.

No, I just want to ask you some questions, about the events of the last couple of days in the lead-up to polling day. Mr Latham, if I could come to you first, just on the subject of the Murray–Darling River system.

L: Five billion.

Mr Howard?

H: Six and a half billion.

Aged care?

L: Ten billion.

H: Twelve billion.

Education?

L: Four billion to state schools.

Mr Howard?

H: Four and a half billion to private schools.

Health. Mr Howard?

H: Nine billion.

Mr Latham?

L: Fifteen billion.

Sport?

L: Six trillion.

H: Eleven trillion.

Roads?

H: Nine billion.

L: 1.75 billion?

The environment?

L: Sixty billion.

H: Sixty-two and a half.

L: Sixty-three.

H: Sixty-three and a half.

L: Sixty-four.

H: Sixty-four and a half.

L: No, I'm out.

I'll take five thousand.

L: No.

Are you all done? Are you all finished? Are you all silent?

L: Yes.

Hang on. I'll just go in and see what my instructions are.

H: Who's the vendor?

I'm just going to see Mr Brown.

H: Who's Mr Brown?

He controls the Upper House. We can't sell without him.

L: Mr Brown?

H: What's the zoning? We can have the zoning changed can't we?

L: Yes. Bryan, we can talk about this. We can call all this a wetland. We'll put an owl breeding hutch down there by the river.

H: The river's not there any more.

L: Where's the river?

H: We sold it.

L: What did you do that for? He's not going to like that.

H: Who's not?

L: Mr Brown. The bloke who lives upstairs.

H: Blast!

THE HON. MARK LATHAM, LEADER OF THE OPPOSITION

In which electoral defeat is interpreted for us by the Hon. Member for Dunkirk

Mr Latham, thanks for your time.
Good to see you, Bryan.
How are you?
Good thanks.
Is the party regrouping?
Regrouping well, yes. We've had a lot of discussions.
What about?
About how we could have gone better. What to do next time. How to build a better party.
Yes, you've got a bit of thinking to do haven't you?
A bit of what?
You've got a lot of thinking to do.
Look I don't want to reveal too much about the way we do things in the ALP.
Should we wait for the others?
What others?
The other senior figures in the party.
I can answer any questions about the party. I'm the leader.
Yes, I want to ask you about the leadership.
I can answer those. Don't try and make trouble. The ALP is in very good order. Every state and territory in the country is run by a Labor government.
Yes, it's the performance of the federal ALP I want to ask about.
Yes. OK. *(Answers phone.)* Hang on. Hello. Yes. At the ABC. No, the ABC. Yes now. Well who told you that?
Who's that?
Bob McMullan. He's gone to the wrong place.
Where is he? We'll send a cab for him.

He's in Adelaide. He wants to know if John Faulkner's here. Do you know a John Faulkner?

Yes. Senator Faulkner. He's not here yet but yes, he's supposed to be talking to us.

Bob. They've never heard of him. Don't worry about it. I'm there now. No, he hasn't asked me anything yet. You rang and interrupted.

Can I talk to him?

Hang on, he wants to talk to you. No, I'm not going to ring Kim if anything tricky crops up. I'll handle it.

(Hands phone over.) **Hello. Bob. Bryan Dawe here. Yes. No, he looks good. They're fine, they're on the right way round. No, he hasn't said anything yet. I haven't asked him anything yet.** *(Hangs up.)*

(Answers phone.) Yes? Sorry, wrong number.

Who was that?

Kim Beazley.

Mr Latham, how do you think things are going?

Very well.

The government's back in office.

They are, but they're selling Telstra, they've got interest rates going up, they're going to attack the workers, the Free Trade Agreement is stalled and Mr Costello says he thinks the Treasury figures were a bit optimistic.

I don't want to talk about the government, I want to talk about the opposition.

I'm your man.

THE HON. PETER COSTELLO, TREASURER OF AUSTRALIA

In which Barnum senses that perhaps he should have a word with Bailey

Mr Costello, thanks for your time.

Thank you for inviting me.

How are things going in the new government?

Good. Should be great. We had the class photo taken the other day.

Who were you sitting next to?

I was next to John Howard. He's the captain and I'm the vice-captain.

John Anderson told me he was the vice-captain.

We let Ando call himself the vice-captain.

Why.

It's Ando's bus that we use to get the team to the ground.

I see, so who is the actual vice-captain?

I am. If the captain decides to retire it won't be John Anderson who takes over the captaincy.

It'll be you.

Yes, so I'm one out and one back and Ando is the vice-captain.

Where's Tony Abbott?

In the photo Tony is just behind me.

What's he doing?

I don't know but I asked him to stop it.

Why?

Because I've never liked knives.

You don't trust them?

I do. I think they're very reliable. I just don't like what they do.

Mr Costello, you've indicated you think some of the Treasury figures provided before the election might have been a bit optimistic.

I have, yes.

What did you mean by that?

Sometimes people, with the best will in the world, get things wrong.

Just before an election.

That's very often the case.

There's a lot of pressure on people at that time, I suppose.

There would be otherwise, yes.

Why didn't you point out to them that you thought they'd got it wrong?

I did.

After the election.

As soon after the six week campaign as possible, I made a public statement.

Is there anything else you didn't point out during the campaign?

No.

Are interest rates going up?

With that exception.

Did you mention the sale of Telstra?

With those exceptions.

Why has the Free Trade Agreement been delayed?

With the exception of these trivialities you mention, I was very clear with the electorate.

OK. This business of the Treasury figures being a bit optimistic before the election.

Yes.

Why was this mistake made?

Because of the emergence of a factor they may not have taken into account, through no fault of their own.

What is it?

Have you got a pencil?

Yes.

Oil prices.

Why are oil prices so high?

International demand is up, driven largely by China.

Isn't the Chinese economy the great growth machine in world economics?

No one told anyone in Treasury.

What's the other reason?

There's a war on in the gulf. That's where a lot of the oil comes from.

Aren't we involved in the war?

Not Treasury, no.

Haven't we got troops there?

Yes. Different department. 'Oil prices'. You've written 'Peter'.

The reason is 'oil prices'.

THE HON. BRENDAN NELSON, MINISTER FOR EDUCATION

In which we are united in our admiration

Brendan Nelson, thanks for your time.

Just relax, Byran. Pace yourself.

You've announced plans to get stuck into the universities.

We've announced plans to reform certain aspects of the tertiary education sector. You see this is where the ABC gets itself into trouble. There's no need to ask that question in that form. I don't know why you do it. It gives you away. You've got an ideological position. You're pretending to be objective. You're working for the national broadcaster.

Who do you work for?

I'm in a different position. I work for the government.

Mr Nelson, I…

No, let me finish, Bryan. You're a public servant. The ABC is owned by the government, by the taxpayers. Ordinary people paying their tax, that's where your bread and butter comes from. Your job, if I might say so, is not to express your own particular poisonous prejudice. It is to make the program in the best interests of the whole of Australia, this is the Australian Broadcasting Corporation.

I understand that.

Well that's good.

May I continue?

You may, but bear in mind the guidelines I've given you.

Certainly. And I thank you for the tips.

Pleasure.

Dr Nelson, you've announced plans to reform certain aspects of the tertiary education sector.

That's right, Bryan, I have.

How are you going to achieve this?

What does it mean in practical terms?

Yes.

We're going to get stuck into the universities, Bryan.

Yes. Why is that, Dr Nelson?

It's ideological. There are ideas being expressed in the universities at the moment that are not the government's.

Hasn't that always been the case?

It has, Bryan. It's taken us a while to wake up to it but we're on to it now.

Are there other places where there are ideas being expressed which aren't the government's?

Outside the universities is the other main venue for dissent.

You believe that the universities should be controlled by the federal government?

I do. *(He looks to the back of the room.)* Who is that giggling? Come on. Share the joke.

Dr Nelson. You've said you don't think university students should have to join a student union.

That's right. I don't think the Australian public wants its money spent on a lot of radicals running about the country doing as they please. *(He looks to the back of the room.)* Who said that's what taxpayers are doing? Who said this government is a bunch of radicals who aren't acting in the best interests of the country. I can wait. I've got all day. This has happened before, hasn't it?

Not since you were here last.

We'll wait, Bryan.

Are we staying in?

Yes. You can bang the dusters together. Come on. Bang bang.

A VOTER

In which we are reminded of a bygone era

Thanks for your time this evening.

Good to be here.

You're the Labor voter.

There's not just me, is there? I thought there were a few of us.

I mean you're the Labor voter we've asked to come in this evening.

Yes.

Are you a member of the party?

Yes. Have been for many years.

Right. Now are you aware of where the party is going?

I'm aware the party is regrouping and is developing new initiatives, new policies, new ideas.

And you are going with them on this journey, are you?

Yes.

Yes. Do you suffer from nose bleeds?

No. Why?

Blood pressure OK?

I think so, why?

Just in case there are any very sharp turns.

Do you think there will be?

I don't know. But strange things are happening. Interest rates are going up.

Yes, that's right. I might take a hat.

And I see Des Moore wants to abolish all unions of any kind.

Yes. I might stick the wet weather gear in.

Brendan Nelson wants to run the university system out of the back of his garage.

Yes, I might take a spare pair of trousers.

I saw the governor-general on the front of the paper the other day talking about abortion rates.

Yes, I saw that.

You don't think that was part of some sort of government move on social policy and women's health.

This is the story where he was standing on the lawn in front of Government House swinging a golf club.

Yes, why would there be a photo of him doing that?

I imagine there just happened to be a photographer passing.

That'll probably be it.

I might take some decompression tablets.

You don't know where the Labor Party is going on these issues?

No. I got a call from Wayne Swan the other night.

What did Wayne say?

He said we were going on a mystery flight.

Did he tell you anything else?

No.

Did they give you a map?

No, we were issued with a life raft and a whistle to attract attention.

Wayne Swan didn't say anything else?

He said he wasn't a rooster any more.

What did that mean?

It could have been the phone line.

But he didn't say where you were going.

No, but he said it was going to be flexible but fair.

How could it be fair if it was flexible?

He didn't say.

How can it be flexible if it's going to be fair?

I don't know.

It could have been the phone line.

Yes. Probably the phone line.

Where was he speaking from?

He was just behind me.

What was he doing?

He was tying my hands up with some phone line.

THE HON. ROBERT HILL, MINISTER FOR DEFENCE

In which every small company will thrill to the example provided by government

Senator Hill, thanks for your time.

Pleasure, Bryan.

You've had a bit of a problem with the accounts in the Defence Department.

Let's be clear about this. The accounts are quite good. A model of their kind.

What kind are they?

Accounts with $8 billion worth of assets missing.

There are no rural grants in these accounts are there?

No, not at all. These are just the accounts of the Australian Defence establishment.

So what's the problem with the accounts?

The problem isn't with the accounts.

So where would an accounting problem be if it weren't in the accounts?

I'm only the minister responsible but it would be in knowing where the things in the accounts actually were.

The assets.

The alleged assets.

Like what?

Defence equipment. Have you seen the budget?

Yes, I've got a copy of it.

If you go to the capital expenditure, you'll find the ordnance is all listed there.

This is the equipment.

Yes. It's all listed under specific headings.

'Things that go "whoosh"?'

Yes. Good example.

'Things that go "kerblam"?'

Yes, different class of weaponry.

'Things that go AWOL'?

They're in a separate schedule.

Where is it? Is it here?

No. We don't know where that is but it'll turn up, it'll be somewhere

'Helicopters we ordered four years ago'?

Yes.

$600 million.

Yes.

Each.

That's right.

Why does it say 'No photo available'?

Because we haven't got the helicopters yet.

We've just paid for them.

That's right. That's the key point. As soon as we get them we'll be out there with the camera.

So these items listed as being 'probably somewhere'?

It's more specific than that, isn't it?

Yes. Sorry. 'Probably somewhere in Australia or Asia or the Middle East.'

Yes.

These are actual weapons are they?

Correct. Top draw stuff too.

But we don't know where they are.

Yes. They'll be somewhere. We just have to find them.

How are you going to do that?

I've been given the name of some people who might be able to help.

Who are they?

There's a guy called Hans Blix.

The weapons inspector?

Yes. Apparently he can go into your country and find weapons.

And you're going to get him to come to Australia and find ours?

Well, we can't find them. We must be practical.

What are they?

The missing items?

Yes. $8 billion worth of what, exactly?

Items defence personnel have mislaid.

What sort of thing?

Some submarines.

Someone's mislaid a submarine?

Yes. Just put one down somewhere.

And forgotten it?

Yes, the phone rang or something.

How do you think the taxpayer feels about all this?

The taxpayer should be very happy.

Why?

The quality of the stuff we can't find is second to none.

Senator Hill, thanks for your time

You haven't got some amphibious tanks have you?

No. Why?

(*Looking around.*) Anyone? Amphibious tanks? Rockets?

HARD TIMES

2005

THE HON. KIM BEAZLEY, LEADER OF THE OPPOSITION

In which we meet an old friend and struggle to master our excitement

Thanks very much for your time.

Very good to be here. Good evening.

You are…Mr?

Kim Beazley.

Kim Beazley. That's right. How are you? I haven't seen you for a bit

No. I'm very well thanks. How are you?

I'm good thanks. Now you're doing the job of…

I'm the leader of the opposition.

Yes. Mark Latham's old job.

Yes. Mark's no longer with the firm.

Where is Mark now?

Mark's working from home.

Who was in Mark Latham's old job before Mark Latham?

The way we look at it, it's not Mark Latham's old job. It's my job.

Yes, but who was in the job before Mark Latham?

Simon Crean was.

And before that?

I was, before that.

And before that?

Before me?

Yes.

Me again. But look, you seem to be concentrating on the past. We're a party of the future. We have a forward-looking view…aren't you going to interrupt me?

No, I was going to see what you had to say.

I haven't got anything to say. I was just making the point that we're the party of the first part

(Helping.) **Of the future.**

Of the future.

My point is that you go back a fair way You were the last leader but two and the last but three.

That's right.

When were the Crusades?

The Crusades were before that. My position is similar to that of John Howard. He had about six goes at being leader before he won an election.

And why was that?

The Liberal Party was shell-shocked. They'd been humiliated in a few elections on the trot. They didn't know what they were…Didn't know how best to get the man obviously best suited to manage the country, into the driver's seat.

You nearly won the federal election in 1998, didn't you?

I did. I came within a…

A win.

I came within a win of winning that one.

And you came within a win of winning again in 2001.

I did. The only thing that preventing us from winning that one was the…

The fact that you had the same policies as the government?

Not so much that but that they had them first.

So you had some bad ideas?

We had plenty of bad ideas.

But you didn't have them first.

That's right, and that told against us.

Did you toy with the prospect of having any good ideas, at any stage?

Yes, I'm pretty sure we looked at that.

Wouldn't work?

I think someone suggested that. Perhaps some of the women.

You don't think it would work?

It wasn't up to me. I was only the leader of the party.

So who runs the party if not the leader?

I've got that here. *(He takes a card from his pocket and reads.)* A bloke called. Who's this? I didn't know there *was* a Rupert Packer.

That's two cards.

I see. *(Off.)* Harry, what's the name of the bloke who ultimately sets ALP policy at the moment. That's it. John Howard.

Thanks for coming in.

THE HON. PETER COSTELLO, TREASURER OF AUSTRALIA

In which we meet the basics and they are us

Mr Costello, thanks for coming in.
Nice to be here, Bryan.

This deficit figure that was announced this week, this is not terribly good news is it?
Do you mind if we don't talk about this? I know you asked if we could…

You were the one who said Australian economic management was so good.
I realise that.

It turns out we've got the biggest deficit in our history.
I realise that.

I mean, either you knew about this before the election, in which case why didn't you do something about it…
I realise it looks bad.

Or you didn't know anything about it, in which case what were you doing?
Yes, can we just not talk about it for a minute? I've had nothing but this for two days.

At the risk of upsetting you, a lot of people are going to lose their houses here.
I know how serious it is. I just want to talk about something else.

OK. Let's talk about health.
Not health.

Education?
No, look we might get on to Brendan Nelson.

Aged care?
Yes fine. What's aged care?

The care of old people.
The care of old people by the rest of the community?

Yes.

No. You've lost me.

Defence?

Not really my area.

Whose is it?

I think it's the Foreign Minister's.

Why not the Minister for Defence?

Because in order to defend ourselves we've had to go to Iraq.

Indigenous Affairs?

That's a good point. We should be able to make some economies there.

How is Australia's record on asylum seekers?

Yes, look we might be best with the economy. What would you like to know?

I think Australians would like to be assured that the Australian economy in good hands.

Yes, it is. I've met many of the people who run it and they seem very good.

What's the problem?

Just debt, really. We're spending too much.

Why?

And we're borrowing too much to do it.

What can be done about it?

And a lot of the money we've been borrowing is invested in housing.

Not a big foreign exchange earner.

Not traditionally, no.

So what are you going to do about it?

I'm going to keep trying to get the message out.

What message?

That it's not happening.

So nothing to worry about.

No. It's good news really. It's the blow-out we needed to have.

(Whoop, whoop.) **What was that?**

Just an alarm of some kind. They must be testing them.

HIS ROYAL HIGHNESS CHARLES WINDSOR, PRINCE OF WALES

In which we trust

Your Highness, thanks for your time tonight.
Not at all. It's good to be here. What do you do?
I'm the person who'll be interviewing you.
I see. That's very interesting. And how long have you been doing that?
Interviewing people? I've been doing it for a number of years.
Really. And what do these other people do?
They're the camera crew.
Really. And how long have they been doing that?
Quite some time, most of them. Your Highness, I wonder if I could ask, do you enjoy coming to Australia?
I love it. I've been here many times, of course.
You went to school here, didn't you?
I went to school here at…
Geelong.
At Geelong.
And you enjoyed that?
Loved it. I remember we went away at one point, to…
Timbertop.
Timbertop. Great days. Marvellous days. It was connected to school down at somewhere or other.
Geelong.
Geelong. Yes, know it well.
You went to school there.
I went to school there.
You've announced you're getting married again.
Yes, that's right.
What has been the reaction to that decision?
Well, happily, she's agreed. So I'm over the first hurdle, which is great.
I mean more generally. What has been the general reaction?

Very good, supportive, people accept one has the right to one's happiness.

What about your mother?

Ah. That has been a slight difficulty.

Because she has said she isn't coming to the wedding, hasn't she?

She has. She wasn't that keen on my first...

Wife?

...experiment in this area. I don't know whether you've read Frood?

Freud?

Austrian chap.

Yes.

Yes, he's very good on this stuff. The whole wife/mother department. Rather a can of worms the whole thing. Would that I had known. If I knew what then I now have known...

Your Royal Highness...

How do you do?

Will you be king?

I'd very much like to be king.

You've trained for it.

I have. I can stand still for hours.

Is it difficult being royal? Is there a lot of pressure?

I've never known anything else.

All the very best.

Thank you for your time.

It's a pleasure. And what do you do?

I'm interviewing you.

And how long have you been doing that?

A NEWSPAPER EDITOR

In which the power and weakness are sometimes confused

Thanks for your time.

No trouble at all.

You run what I suppose we can call a major daily newspaper.

Certainly. One of the big four.

Which are the big four?

Ourselves and the three other big ones.

And how are things going in the media at the moment?

They're going pretty well. Advertising revenues are up. We're certainly going well.

And what are the big stories at the moment?

The big news stories?

Yes.

You've got your Danish Prince and Princess…

This is Mary, the girl from Tasmania?

Yes, our Mary. A fabulous story.

It is a great story, isn't it?

It's a dream story. It's got elements of reality and fantasy.

He seems so nice too, doesn't he?

He does. Everyone likes him. A marvellous story.

And they've been in Sydney of course.

They have charmed Sydney.

Yes. What else?

Well yes, there are other stories of course. You've got your Danish royals. They're in Melbourne now.

Yes, I mean apart from the Danish royals, what other stories are big in Australia at the moment?

Plenty of other stuff; Prince Charles, Delta, someone hacked into Paris Hilton's phone, we're doing a thing on where to get the best coffee, shoes…

What's happening in the Middle East?

House prices, yes, they certainly seem to have stabilised.

No I mean in Iraq.

Iraq?

Yes.

Something about Syria.

Yes, what about Syria?

I think George Bush has warned Syria.

What about?

Warned them to stop doing that thing they were doing.

What will he do if they don't stop?

I imagine he'll go in there and bring freedom and democracy to the Syranians.

How do you think the Australian economy is going?

It's going well. As I say, advertising revenues are up. We're making a poultice…

I mean the broader economy.

Advertising revenue is up across the board. I don't know anyone who's not making a quid out of advertising revenue.

Do you think there'll be another interest rate hike?

Not before Gallipoli. We've pretty much got the Gallipoli coverage organised. They'd be mad to get in the road of that.

How do you think the poor are travelling in this country at the moment?

The poor? Look, I'll be honest, we don't cover a lot of stories about the poor.

Why not?

It's difficult to interest the advertisers in buying space in a story about the poor.

What about the sick? The health system doesn't work.

Yes, not news really if it's not working.

Or the aged?

No, you can hook them in on the Old Folks if there's a nice retirement development being released. 'Calming Vistas', 'Autumnal Heights' or something.

And what would you run there?

We wouldn't just be running the press handout, if that's what you're asking.

What would you be running?

We'll be running the press handout, but you can just cut at my last answer.

This is live.

We're going out live?

Yes.

(Off.) Get me a big picture of Prince Frederick and Our Mary, will you?

THE HON. MALCOLM TURNBULL, PARLIAMENTARY SECRETARY TO THE PRIME MINISTER

In which we see that if time is being bided, there may be an anxiety about place

Mr Turnbull, thanks for your time.
Good evening, Bryan.

You've been in some trouble with your party leadership this week.
Only because they've got no idea what they're doing.

Why don't they know what they're doing?
They're completely out of touch. They've got no idea. Some of these people have never had a proper job.

You've been particularly critical of the government's tax policy.
Yes. Can we swap seats?

No, I think I'll stay here. Mr Turnbull, you've been critical of the government's tax policy.
The whole country is critical of it. Why wouldn't they be. We've got the highest taxes in our history and some of the richest people aren't paying any tax at all *(He moves closer.)*

What are you doing?
I'm working for tax reform. *(He moves closer.)*

Can you get back over there?
Back where?

Back to where you were.
I thought it would be better if we were together.

I prefer you over there. Mr Turnbull, you're in an odd position here, aren't you?
Yes, I'd rather be over there.

What I mean is, you're part of the government.
That's right.

So what do you say to people who say your primary loyalty is to the party?

My primary loyalty is obviously to the country and if my party is
doing something counterproductive and very stupid, like taxing some
of them to the point where they can't afford to stay in business and
leaving corporate loopholes you could drive a truck through, then I'll
say so.

**My point is that at the moment you're doing more damage to the
government than the opposition is.**

I'm opposed to what the government is doing. What do you expect me
to do? Sit there and do nothing like Costello and Hill and these other
laureates?

My point is...

I reckon you'd be better here.

I'm happy here, thanks.

(To cameraman.) On me a bit more thanks. If Bryan's saying something
interesting by all means cut to him. But if he isn't, keep it on me. I'm
the talent.

**Mr Turnbull. The director of the show will decide who the camera
should be on.**

On me.

Mr Turnbull.

Can I speak to the director of the *(To Bryan)* what's the show called?
(He dials a phone number.)

7.30 Report.

Director of 'The 7.30 Report' please. Yes. I'll wait. On me. I know who
I'll ring.

(Kerry O'Brien closes the show. As he does so, his phone starts ringing.)

THE HON. JOHN HOWARD, AMANDA VANSTONE AND ALEXANDER DOWNER

In which a great idea fails to rate because the contestants don't know what they're doing. Such a shame. Could've been great

Thank you all for coming. Let's test those buzzers. John Howard. *(Buzz)* **Amanda Vanstone.** *(Clang)* **Alexander Downer.** *(Buzz)* **OK. What is this sound?** *(Bombs being dropped.)* *(Buzz)* **Mr Downer?**

D: Freedom and democracy.

Can you be more specific?

D: Can we hear it again?

Yes, let's hear it again. What is this sound? *(Bombs being dropped.)* *(Buzz)* **Mr Downer?**

D: Is it peace breaking out in Afghanistan?

(Buzz) **Mr Howard?**

H: Is it an election in Iraq?

No. Listen again. *(Bombs being dropped.)* *(Buzz)* **Mr Downer?**

D: Is it a peaceful transition of power in Syria or hasn't that happened yet? *(Clang)*

Amanda Vanstone?

V: Have we started yet? I can't hear anything.

Yes, we've started. Listen again. *(Bombs being dropped.)* *(Buzz)* **Mr Howard?**

H: It's obviously peace and democracy. The question is where *(Buzz)*

Mr Downer?

D: Wherever George says. *(Buzz)*

Mr Howard?

H: Can we phone a friend?

No. You haven't got a friend, Mr Howard. *(Clang)* **Amanda Vanstone?**

V: Can I hear the sound please? I haven't heard anything yet.

Yes. Let's try a different one. *(Someone being hit or moaning in pain.)* *(Buzz)* **Mr Downer?**

D: Someone being interviewed. *(Buzz)*

Mr Howard?

H: Is it something to do with education?

No. It's not to do with education although that's a very good answer. *(Clang)* **Amanda Vanstone?**

V: Have we heard the sound yet?

Yes, we have but here it is again. *(Someone being hit.)* *(Buzz)* **Mr Howard?**

H: Is it a small business enjoying the benefits of the GST?

No. Let's try another one *(Clang)* **Amanda Vanstone?**

V: When's lunch? I'm starving.

We're nearly finished. Here is the final sound. *(Splash)* *(Buzz)* **Mr Howard?**

H: Is that an election being called?

Not quite. *(Buzz)* **Mr Downer?**

D: Children being thrown in the sea by their own parents?

Nearly. *(Clang)* **Amanda Vanstone?**

V: Peter Reith getting a job in Europe?

No. And at the end of that round John's team has complete control of the Senate. *(An intruder walks into the picture.)* **Who are you?**

I'm an Australian voter.

Hang on. Security!

THE HON. TONY ABBOTT, MINISTER FOR HEALTH AND AGEING

In which a man is put in the difficult position of being questioned

Mr Abbott, thanks for your time.

Pleasure.

You've said that you were disappointed that the government's promise in relation to the Medicare safety net had been broken.

I was, yes.

Why?

Well I'm the Health Minister. It could look as if I'm responsible.

For Health?

Yes.

Yes, it's a mistake the community could easily make.

That's right.

I can see that, yes. Does it upset you that another one of the government's promises has been broken?

Yes. Oh you're serious.

Yes.

Can you ask me the question again?

Does it upset you that another one of the government's promises has been broken?

Yes it does, although you sometimes don't know when you make a promise, that later on you're going to find that all the figures are wrong and you can't deliver.

So why make the promise?

Yes, well that's what's so upsetting.

If your figures were wrong the first time, what other figures did you have wrong at that time.

Yes, well that's all coming out too. It's very embarrassing.

You said you thought of resigning.

I did, yes.

Briefly.

It crossed my mind, yes.

Why?

For the reasons I outlined. I was the minister. We got it wrong. We went to the electorate. We presented a position and now we're presenting a different one and people are going to have to pay a lot more to go to the doctor.

So you considered resigning from the government?

I did.

Briefly.

Yes.

OK, when was this?

What's that?

This is a printout of your electro-neurological impulses over the last few months.

Good heavens.

When was it you considered resigning?

It was about a week ago. Quite recently.

Is this it? There's a little bump here.

No. That's an interview with Tony Jones, see that's late at night.

What's this here?

That's me preparing a press release.

What's this?

The press release catching fire.

Where's the moment when you considered resigning?

Is this it?

No, that's a full stop.

Is that it?

No that's the dot above this i here.

I definitely considered resigning.

Because you were so upset.

Yes. It'll be here somewhere.

Can we get a microscope?

Yes, and a pen.

THE HON. JOHN HOWARD, PRIME MINISTER OF AUSTRALIA

In which mateship is seen as a useful sedative

Mr Howard, thanks for your time.
Nice to be talking to you.

Yes, there's been some discussion about Anzac Day this year, hasn't there?
Yes, there has, Bryan, and I've made my position as plain as I can get it. I support those Australians who were there at Gallipoli. I don't have a problem with their behaviour. I was proud to be their commanding officer.

Mr Howard, I was actually meaning the meaning of Anzac Day altogether.
I've seen it said that they perhaps got on the turps and left some crap lying about on the peninsula, but they are Australians. I mean, you get with your mates, you have a couple and lose track of what's going on and you make a bit of a bloody mess. We do that at home, Bryan. I don't see the difference.

Mr Howard, I wondered if the meaning of Anzac Day has somehow changed?
Anzac Day is a day of great importance in the Australian calendar, Bryan.

What do you think that importance is?
Well, I think the essential lessons and characters of Anzac Day are as they have always been, Bryan.

And what are they?
Well, it celebrates that very important time when the Australian government made a very significant decision, Bryan to…

To do as it was told by an imperial power.
…to assemble a very, very impressive body of young men, very talented, very resourceful young men and to send them away to…

Invade another country.

…to defend Britain.

By invading Turkey.

And the way they did it, Bryan, was of the utmost importance because for a start they were…

Landed in a wrong place.

…as I say, a very resourceful group of people. When you try to get into the AIF in the very first lot of volunteers, Bryan, you couldn't get in if you were under six foot one so, obviously our…

Graves were a little longer.

…army was a very impressive body of men and they were led by generals who were…

On a boat a couple of miles off the coast.

…dealing with a pretty significant problem. I mean they had a difficult task. That terrain—I've been over the land, Bryan, and it's very difficult land. I've done that, and a lot of the generals at the time…

Hadn't bothered to…

…they weren't given that opportunity because they were obviously…

Tucking into a bit of dinner.

…trying to deal with the bigger picture and there was a bigger picture because Anzac Day doesn't only celebrate Gallipoli. I mean, the First World War, Bryan, is full of other…

Cock-ups.

…very, very famous battles and this is where Australia comes of age. This is where we stand astride centre stage and become a nation. I mean, obviously the empire is not there any more. We're in charge of our own destiny now. Now when Australia wants to know what it's doing in the future it certainly doesn't look to Britain. What we do now is…

Ring George.

…hang on, I've got to ring George. I just got a message to ring George.

No, Prime Minister, that was me.

The important thing, Bryan, is that Anzac Day is very, very, very important to all…

Politicians.

Almost sacred, you might say, Bryan, to all…

Advertising sales.

…to all Australians.

Prime Minister, thanks for your time.

Yes, good on you. Now bugger off, I'm going to talk to George, Bryan, about Australia. We'll let you know. *(Into phone.)* George, John Howard. Howard.

THE HON. JOHN HOWARD AND PETER COSTELLO

In which the headmaster confronts matters head-on

All right. Sit down, the pair of you. Goodness gracious me. How many times do we have to have this conversation? I've got you both in here together and you are staying in after school until we sort this matter out. Now, Peter, what is going on?

P: Nothing.

Peter, please don't tell me nothing is going on. I saw the two of you speaking to each other the way you did the other day. Now, it's just not good enough. Everyone heard it. John, what is going on?

J: I wasn't here the other day. I was, er, down the shops.

You weren't down the shops, John, you were here—I saw you. Look, the problem we've got here is you are both senior boys. Do you understand the effect this is going to have on some of the young ones if they see what you are doing? Now, Peter, what is going on?

P: Well, John won't let me have a go on the bike. Everyone knows it's my turn next. It's on the noticeboard. It's been on the noticeboard for ages and he goes round and round and round. He's selfish. He's never going to give me a go on the bike. I'm never going to get a go on the bike now.

J: You don't even know how to have a go on the bike. I mean, it's no use you saying you want to go on the bike. You keep saying you want a go on the bike. It's no use if I'm really good at going on the bike and I pull over and give it to you and you go and hit a wall because you don't even know what you're doing on the bike. That's no use at all.

P: You said you would give me a go on the bike.

All right, boys.

J: Well, I will. I just haven't finished yet. I will give you a go.

P: You're never going to finish. You just said you'd give me a go on the bike so I don't push you off.

All right, boys.

J: You couldn't push a pumpkin down a hill, you great puff-ball.

Boys! Boys!

P: You're an idiot.

J: You stink.

P: Your bum sticks out, anyway.

All right. Listen. Enough is enough. I expected a little bit more maturity particularly from you, John. Please. Are you going to give Peter a go on the bike at some stage?

J: Yes.

Well, when?

J: Later.

P: Yes, what does that mean? I'm never going to get a go on the bike. *(Repeats.)* I'm never going to get a go on the bike!

Listen, stop it. OK. I'll tell you what concerns me about this, both of you. It is this: while you've been arguing, a truck has driven over the oval, there are big skid marks everywhere. On top of that, the goal posts are missing, and the science block has burnt down. Incidentally, do either of you boys know a boy called Downer?

J: No.

P: No.

Well, he's got his head stuck in the toilet. I've rung Mr Kyoto, I've rung Mr Hicks and Mr Corby. I can't get in contact with any of them. And the bank manager, on top of all this, has rung and said we're $5 billion in debt.

J: Well, Peter…

And I don't know what you boys think you are doing, but I'm just about sick of both of you. Get out!

J: Do you want a go on the bike?

P: No, it's your bike.

Go on, clear off! I'm sick of the both of you. Turnbull! Tell Malcolm to get in here, will you. Hurry up!

J: Turnbull?

P: Turnbull?

J: Bloody hell.

THE HON. KIM BEAZLEY, LEADER OF THE OPPOSITION

In which home again home again jiggeddy-jig

Mr Beazley, thanks for your time.

It's a great pleasure to be on the program, Bryan, and thank you very much.

Yes. It's a pleasure. You said you'd be voting against the tax cuts.

Yes. Can I just change that answer, because…

Well, no, it's a matter of public record, Mr Beazley.

Does that matter? I mean, it doesn't matter when the government changes its mind. John Howard announces a policy, waits for the lights to change and then announces a new policy which is the opposite of his first policy.

Yes, but you keep agreeing with him.

It's a bit hard not to. He's adopted both positions, Bryan. He's saying both things. Everything I say will agree with one of his positions, either the one that he's discarded or the one that he's adopted.

But, Mr Beazley, what about these immigration foul-ups? These are Australian citizens. They have Australian passports and you're not saying anything.

That's right. But let me just say this, Bryan, because…

Hang on a second. I thought you said you had nothing to say.

The point I'm making here, Bryan—and I'd like people to be very clear about this—is that this is not the *only issue* on which I've got nothing to say.

There are other matters you have nothing to say about?

Oh, yes. There are a large range of issues, Bryan, on which that is our policy.

Mr Beazley, if you're going to say nothing about something, why don't you just go and say it?

Well, because you're making it a little bit difficult at the moment. I'm struggling to get it out, Bryan.

I'm sorry. I'm not trying to interrupt you or stop you from saying what you want to say.

You might not be doing it intentionally, Bryan, but you are interrupting me, and you have been since the beginning of this discussion.

Mr Beazley, how can I be interrupting you? You said you had nothing to say.

I haven't, Bryan, but for goodness' sake let me get it out!

Mr Beazley, I don't understand your point.

Bryan, what we've got in this country is that we've got this government, this John Howard government, which says one thing to the Australian people and it does another.

And what is your position on this?

Our position, Bryan, is that we're not just saying nothing…

You're doing nothing.

…we're *doing* nothing.

Right. Consistency.

Consistency is our watchword, Bryan. We are a model of consistency, and we will continue to be a model of consistency…

(Bryan is on the phone, placing bets.) **Race 4, No. 7? Yes.**

…and I think that's, as much as anything else, what people are looking for in an opposition. They don't want shillyshallying. They want certainty. They want to know what the position is, and they want to see it consistently articulated.

Port Adelaide by 20 points against Essendon.

That is what we have been doing, and, in fact, anybody who doesn't think we'll be doing that is making a very grave error, Bryan.

Probably Cronulla.

A very grave error, and I tell you what I'd say to this government. I would say to this government: you want rhetoric? We'll give you rhetoric!

No, no, Brumbies for the win; they've got to win sooner or later.

We'll give you rhetoric. Stand back and watch this! You want rhetoric? That's what I'd say to them, Bryan.

No, no, no, I'm at work. Yes, no, I'm trying to do an interview with

Kim Beazley.

Because what we're doing is offering the Australian population, Bryan, a very, very clear option.

Nothing.

Can we get a tank, Bryan? I think some of this argument of mine would go a little bit better if we had some ordnance just in shot.

Mr Beazley, thanks for joining us.

A big tank.

I'll get back to you.

Big tank. Got a tank?

No, we're out of tanks.

Rifles? Anything? A weapon of some kind. Anyone got a biro?

A MINISTERIAL REPRESENTATIVE

In which a man goes out of his way to help

Thanks for coming in.

It's very good to be here. Thank you.

You're not Amanda Vanstone, are you?

Am I Amanda Vanstone? No, I'm not really.

I thought we had arranged to speak to Amanda Vanstone.

Yes, well, the minister is very busy and I've been asked to pop in here and fill in for her.

I don't think we were told that.

I'm telling you now.

But we weren't told beforehand.

Well, I can't help that, sunshine. I'm telling you now, though. I didn't know about it a long time ago myself, to be honest.

What happened?

I was in the office. I got a call from the Minister saying would I get down here and talk to—are you Barry O'Brien?

Bryan Dawe.

Whatever—about whatever particular bee you've got in your bonnet tonight.

We asked the Minister, Amanda Vanstone, to come here specifically and talk about reconciliation and the response was that she was going to be here and that she was keen to discuss these issues.

Good response, too, but something's cropped up. The Minister is very busy.

Well, where is she?

Aside from anything else, she is the Minister for Popping Small Children in the Jail.

She said she would be here at ten to eight.

Yes but something has cropped up and I am here to deputise for her.

Well, where has she gone?

She is at a 'Bring and Buy' in Braidwood, a very important party function. She is yanking a number out of a hat at quarter to nine. She cannot be here!

So this is more important than Aboriginal reconciliation?

Barry, what I'm saying to you...

Bryan.

Mmm?

Bryan.

Whatever. What I'm saying to you is I'm here to help. Ask me any questions. That's what I'm here to deal with.

How high a priority for the government is Aboriginal reconciliation?

Is what?

Aboriginal reconciliation—how high a priority is it?

Oh, you know, pretty high.

Pretty high?

Yes, fairly high. I've heard it mentioned. I've heard the adults talking about it in the other room.

This is ridiculous. You are saying that you've heard reconciliation discussed in an office somewhere?

Yes.

You're not serious about this at all. You've got no interest in it.

Don't patronise me, Barry.

Bryan.

Don't patronise me...Sonny, because I am down here. I should be at a life drawing class. Do you think I like coming down here? There are plenty of people the minister could have sent along here who are much more junior to me in the department. Don't you tell me the minister is not serious about...

Aboriginal reconciliation.

Whatever.

Can you tell me what the minister thought of the remarks of the governor-general this week and the remarks of the governor of Western Australia?

She would probably have been in broad agreement with them, yes.

With whom?

Well, what's the difference?

(*Off.*) **Shane, this is pointless. Well, how are you on immigration?**

Well, give us a run. I can give you a personal opinion on immigration.

Why not? You're missing out on life drawing.

Exactly. I support the Irish guy, Peter O'George.

Petro Georgiou.

Him as well. With them both. I hope that they get a very good hearing in this community.

Really? Why is that?

Because they're going to get rolled in the Parliament. I reckon give them an airing now and we'll put the idea to sleep when it gets to the Senate.

Sorry about the life drawing class.

Well, bugger you, too.

THE HON. PHILIP RUDDOCK, ATTORNEY GENERAL

In which Bryan appears in panto, to excellent effect

Mr Ruddock, thanks for your time.

A very good evening to you, Bryan.

I wonder if I could ask you about this new legislation that's coming in.

Yes, this is the anti-terrorist legislation?

Yes.

Yes, that legislation has been on the books for some time.

These are amendments, aren't they?

We are bringing in some amendments, yes.

And what is the purpose of them?

Well, we will be giving the authorities certain powers, Bryan, the better to defend Australia from terrorism.

What sort of powers, exactly?

They'll be able to enter premises, for example, where they think there might be terrorist activity.

And arrest people?

And arrest people, by all means. We hope they will, yes.

And what will they arrest them for?

Well, they might, for example, think they know something.

They might know what?

Something maybe they shouldn't know, Bryan.

What sort of thing?

That's not specified in the legislation. This would be a matter for them.

So, they could arrest me?

Theoretically, Bryan, yes, if they thought you perhaps knew something.

What sort of thing would I know?

As I say, Bryan, this is not specified in the legislation. This would be a matter for the arresting officer.

But, Mr Ruddock, how would I establish my innocence here?

Well, you wouldn't be innocent, Bryan, if you were being arrested, would you? They are not going to arrest you if you are innocent.

They're not fools, these people.

How do I get out of this?

You'd have to establish, in some persuasive way, that perhaps the thing that they thought you knew, you don't know.

How do I do that?

I have no idea, Bryan. That's not my problem.

But I would have to prove that I didn't know it.

That's it. It's fairly simple.

But isn't that the opposite of the presumption of innocence?

Bryan, this is not a normal situation.

In what way isn't it a normal situation, Mr Ruddock?

Someone has come into your house, Bryan, and arrested you because they think you might know something.

Yes, and it's up to me and I have to prove that I don't know it.

That's correct. It's not a normal situation.

Do they tell me what it is that I don't know?

No, they're not going to tell you what it is.

Why not?

Bryan, if I came into your house and arrested you because I thought you might know something, I wouldn't be able to tell you what it is without impeding your capacity to argue that you didn't know what it was.

In that case perhaps no arrest should be made until the alleged offence can be established, Mr Ruddock.

We don't want them to know. We're not going to tell them, Bryan.

But if you don't tell them what it is, how can they possibly argue that they didn't know it? They don't know what it is, Mr Ruddock.

That's right. I think you'll find we've got them there, Bryan. I don't think they've got a leg to stand on, myself, and they deserve everything they've got coming.

When is this legislation coming in?

After 1 July, when we don't have to trouble the scorer much. We'll run both houses.

And you wrote this?

I'm not alone, Bryan. There were several of us there.

Who?

Oh, there was me, Lewis Carroll, a bloke called Escher from South Australia; a few of us.

Do you know what I think of this legislation, Mr Ruddock?

Be a bit careful here, Bryan.

Do you know what I think of this legislation?

Be a bit careful what you say.

(Public announcement.) Bryan Dawe, to the front desk, please. There are some gentlemen here to see you.

Don't look at me, Bryan. You got yourself into this.

ANOTHER 'MASTERMIND' CONTESTANT

In which his own petard is well beaten and lucky to run a place

Okay. Our next contestant. Your name is Peter?

Yes, that's right, yes.

What do you do, Peter?

I'm a Treasurer.

A treasurer. My, that must be an interesting job, is it?

Yes, it can be a bit repetitive sometimes. I actually wouldn't mind becoming a prime minister at some point.

Well good luck, Peter. Your special subject tonight is right-wing incidents in the life of Christ.

That's correct.

Your time starts now. Name one right-wing incident in the life of Christ.

He threw the money lenders out of the temple.

Can you be more specific?

Yes. He went into the temple and there were money lenders there and he became very angry and tipped their tables over and told them they were usurers and threw them out; biffed them out of the place altogether; threw them out of the temple.

What I meant was, how was that a right-wing thing to do?

Yes, I see. It probably isn't, is it?

Can you think of anything else, Peter?

Yes. He fed 4000 people at one time by sharing food.

How much did he charge for that food?

No, he didn't charge for the food, Bryan. He shared his food. They were hungry and he broke up food. It was loaves and fishes. You've probably heard the story.

I know the story. I'm trying to find the right-wing element in feeding people who need food.

Yes, I see. There probably isn't one, is there? He healed the sick.

Yes.

But actually I think he probably did that for nothing. In fact, I think he probably did that because he loved mankind.

It's not really a right-wing mantra, is it?

It's not a *central* tenet of capitalism, the laying on of hands, no.

He made the lame walk, too, didn't he?

He did, and he forgave the people who killed him.

Did he stick any people in detention centres?

Oh, no, I don't think he would have approved of that at all. He got one bloke up from the dead. A bloke was dead and he made him walk.

This is Lazarus?

Lazarus. Yes. He healed him completely. I don't think he would have approved of putting people in a detention centre, no.

Peter, would you like to reconsider your special subject tonight; right-wing incidents in the life of Christ...

No thanks. I'll think of something, Bryan. I'll have to come up with something sooner or later.

Why is that?

Oh, for this other project I'm working on.

You've snookered yourself a bit here, Peter, haven't you?

No, Bryan. I know! He said at one stage it would be as difficult for a rich man to enter the kingdom of heaven as it would be for a camel to pass through the eye of a needle.

Oh, I'll have to check that with the adjudicator, Peter. Hang on. Can we accept that? Yes, sure. Hang on, I'll ask. Peter, what is your net worth?

(Peter is appalled and realises he cannot win.)

THE HON. BARNABY JOYCE

In which Harry Potter describes his first few days at sea

Barnaby Joyce, thanks for your time.
Hello. You're Bryan, aren't you?
I am, yes.
Yes. I've seen you on television. This is great.
You've had quite a baptism of fire this week.
It has been a bit of a lively week for me, yes. Incident-packed.
Will you be going with the headgear?
Certainly I'll be going with the mouthguard in future, Bryan, and
some sort of protection, I think, around the ovipositor. It got a bit
dangerous for a while there.
Did you expect that sort of reception?
I expected a rigorous debate, Bryan, and that's of course what we've
been enjoying, yes.
And had you ever met Bill Heffernan before?
I hadn't ever met Bill Heffernan personally, Bryan, and I look forward
to speaking to him again when he's feeling a bit better.
Oh, you don't think he's well?
He's not at all well, no. He described to me rather a worrying, delirious
kind of dream and then when I went to discuss it with him he spoke
into his lapel and he said, 'He's coming towards me, John, what the hell
do I do now?'
And he came at you with a big stick, didn't he?
Well, I don't think he understood quite what I was saying. That was
the problem.
And what were you saying?
I was saying what I've been saying all along, Bryan; namely, that the
full sale of Telstra won't go ahead unless we get a $2 billion package to
address issues of technology in the bush.
And what are these issues?
We'll find the issues. You give us the dough, we'll come up with the
issues. Don't you worry about that.

Oh, this is Queensland, yes, I'm sorry.

Yes. We'll find the issues, you just get the money. And a truck.

Barnaby, isn't there any other bush in other states?

No, the bush is in Queensland, Bryan.

None in Victoria, Western Australia, South Australia?

No, no. The bush is in Queensland. That's where the money needs to be spent, Bryan. Have a look at the map. The bush is in Queensland.

This is a map of your electorate.

Yes, which is in Queensland, Bryan. It's in the bush. My electorate.

So, Barnaby Joyce, how do you respond to being told to shut up and do the government's bidding?

Well, Bryan, if the Senator for Barking Moron wishes to suggest I will not be representing the people of Queensland he's made a very, very serious error. That's what I'd say to him.

And of course you've told him that.

I did. I told him that. Yes, I was a little briefer with him than that in order to save time. I told him to stick his...

Yes, but you then got described by the Independent Senator for Cutsnake as a dopey so-and-so, didn't you?

I did, Bryan. But these things don't worry me because they're not going to change our policy and our policy is different from the government's. Were that not the case, Telstra wouldn't be the basket case it is and the good folk of Queensland would have elected a spokesmodel from the Liberal Party which they didn't do. They elected me, Bryan.

OK. Barnaby Joyce, what are the key points of your argument?

$2 billion.

This is how Telstra services are going to be improved in the bush?

Yes, $2 billion.

What about other issues?

$2 billion should cover that, Bryan.

Regional health?

$2 billion, I would think.

And what about student union membership, are you concerned about that?

We are, very much so.

And what are you going to do about it?

$2 billion.

Barnaby Joyce, thanks for your time.

$2 billion, Bryan.

A 'MASTERMIND' WINNER

In which Shakespearean tragedy is available in binary form at last

Your special subject is Australian government policy. Your time starts now. Official government policy is to sell Telstra?

Correct.

Or to retain ownership of the half they still own?

Correct.

For two different prices.

Correct.

To the people who already own it.

Correct.

Against the wishes of the Australian public.

Do you mean all of the Australian public?

I mean the great majority. Australia is a democracy.

(Guessing.) Correct.

Did the government put any condition on the sale?

Yes, but they did it anyway.

Correct. What was the condition?

That telephone services be improved in the bush.

Correct. And did they improve the services in the bush?

Sorry, can you repeat the question?

Can you be more specific?

I can hardly hear you.

Correct. What did Telstra used to spend its money on?

On research and development in telephony.

What did it spend its money on in recent years?

On returning a dividend to shareholders.

Correct. Why is Telstra not worth as much money as the government thought it was?

Because it has missed the boat on the new developments in technology and telephony.

Correct. Why?

Because it didn't spend enough money on research and development.

Correct. Why not?

Because it's been spending its money on returning a dividend to shareholders.

Correct. Why can't the government force Telstra to provide a proper service to the Australian public?

Telstra's a public company.

Correct. Why can't Telstra concentrate on the services where the money really is?

Because it's run by the government.

Correct. Who is Telstra's biggest shareholder?

The government.

Correct. Why?

Because they can't afford to sell it.

Correct. Why did they want to sell it in the first place?

Pass.

'To give Australians an opportunity to purchase a stake in this great national institution.'

(Snorts.) That can't be right—it's completely stuffed!

Hang on a sec. *(Seeks an adjudication.)* **Tony, can we accept 'stuffed'?**

T: Bloody oath we can; we were opposed to it in the first place and now it doesn't work as a service and it's missed the boat as a company.

(Both.) **Correct!**

MR MARK LATHAM

In which anything could happen

Mr Latham, thanks for your time.
Nice to be with you, Bryan. How are you?
I'm good, thank you.
Good on you, Bryan.
Gee, you've cut quite a swathe this week.
I don't know about a swathe, Bryan, but I've certainly cut a bit of a swathe during the week.
It's a tough business, isn't it, politics?
I don't know about tough, Bryan, but I'll tell you something about this business, it's pretty tough. Pretty tough.
Didn't you know it was going to be tough when you went into it, though?
Yes, yes. You don't go into a business like this, Bryan, without knowing it's going to be tough. I knew it would be tough. I knew it would be tough. I knew it would be tough.
Did anything surprise you about it, though?
Only the toughness, Bryan. Only the toughness.
But you would have expected that, wouldn't you?
I did. You don't go into a business like this, Bryan, without knowing what to expect.
But were you surprised when it turned out to be so tough?
I wasn't surprised in the sense that it surprised me.
It's just that you didn't expect it?
Exactly. Exactly. Exactly, Bryan. Exactly.
Mr Latham, when did you first realise they were all against you?
When they made me leader of the Labor Party.
And who did that?
They all did. The whole bloody lot of them. They all got together, all of them, literally all of them. And they ganged up on me. They made me the bloody leader of the Labor Party.
And did you expect that?
Well, not to the extent that it happened, Bryan, no.

Did you *want* to be leader of the Labor Party?

Well, I was in the party forever, Bryan. I've been in the party for years and years and years and years and years and years and years and years.

A long time?

So in a way it was kind of an honour to lead these scum.

So you were proud?

I don't know about proud, Bryan, but I tell you something, it makes you proud when it happens. It makes you proud when it happens.

And who was there when they chose you?

Well, there was a bunch of us there. There was me, Dinsdale Piranha and a bloke called Kierkegaard who just sat there biting the heads off whippets.

Kim Beazley?

Beazer was there. Wayne Swan was there. Good to see Barry Hall in the team, isn't it? Good to see Barry got off. Isn't that good news?

Yes. Different sort of Swan, though.

Yes, but it's good to see a bloke getting off a charge of clouting people. I reckon that's quite good.

Oh, you like that?

That's the Australian way for my money, Bryan. That's the Australian way, isn't it?

Mark Latham, thank you very much for your time. Good luck with the book and thanks for coming in.

Yes, well, you can start any time you like now, Bryan.

Pardon?

Ready to roll when you are, Bryan.

We just finished.

Yes, but you don't know what you want to say until it's all over, do you? It doesn't matter until it stops mattering. You don't know what you're going to say until you finish doing the stuff. (*Looking away.*) You see that bloke over there?

Yes.

That's me.

(*Concerned for Mr Latham's health, Bryan wraps it up.*) **Right. Thanks for your time.**

MR R.J. HAWKE,
PREVIOUS TITLEHOLDER

In which we meet an old friend. Because he wants to

Mr Hawke, thanks for coming in.
Very good to see you, Bryan. Very good to see you.
Yes. How have you been? It's lovely to see you again.
Haven't seen you for ages. You're looking well.
It's been a long while, hasn't it?
You're looking a million dollars.
Thank you. What have you been doing?
I live a very varied life. I've got a lot of business interests. Have you
seen *Willy Wonka and the Chocolate Factory?*
Yes.
I get a run there. I have a pretty good life, Bryan, and I'm doing nicely.
**And you've still got it, haven't you? I mean, you can still be part of the
debate when you decide to be.**
I like to think so. And I think it's a sign of maturity in a society that it
can take counsel from former leaders.
Except Mark Latham, of course?
I think you have to draw the line somewhere. A proper verb in the
occasional sentence is often a useful guide.
**Although Kim Beazley didn't think much of your idea about us
becoming a nuclear waste dumping ground, did he?**
I think Kim's point is that's not currently Labor Party policy.
Has the Labor Party got a policy?
That's something you'd need to check with Kim. In any case, I'm
not recommending that we do it, I'm recommending we look very
carefully at the *possibility* of doing it.
Why?
I think someone is going to make a lot of money internationally out of
solving this nuclear waste problem.
But Mr Hawke, isn't it poisonous?

Only for the first four million years.

Isn't that a concern?

It is, but that's why there's a quid in it for the people that work out how to do it, Bryan. It's a big international problem.

Why do you think we can do this?

I think we're very well situated. We're a very big country.

Yes, we are a big country.

We're a very big country, Bryan.

Where would you put it, though?

Let's be clear about this. It needs to be put down a hole.

Have we got holes?

Oh yes, we've got plenty of holes.

This is in the outback?

Absolutely. Have you been out there? Plenty of holes. There are holes everywhere out there.

And where did we get the holes from?

We made the holes digging the uranium out in the first place.

What we do is we get the poisonous waste and pop it down where the uranium came from.

Yes, that's what you do. With the right safety precautions.

Sure, sure. Like what sort of thing?

You know the way you get a bit of cotton wool on the top of a jar of tablets? Put a bit of cotton wool down on the top and ram it down pretty firmly.

Screw the top over.

Screw the top down very firmly, yes. Very firmly, Bryan.

And stand well back.

No, there won't be anyone out there. This is way out in the bush, this is in the desert.

There's nothing out there?

Nothing out there, absolutely nothing there.

Just air.

A bit of air, obviously.

Water?

Possibly some water if it rains.

And land?

Land, obviously the holes are in the land.

And a little bit of cotton wool.

And a little bit of cotton wool. But nothing else out there at all.

So it's pretty safe.

Safe as a church.

Nothing toxic could leak out?

No, and if anything toxic did leak out it wouldn't hurt people or animals or nature unless it was carried by the air or by the water.

The way disease is.

The way diseases are, yes. But I think it's pretty unlikely.

Why is that?

If the cotton wool is rammed down firmly enough, it's not going to happen, Bryan, don't worry about it.

Have you got any shares in nuclear waste disposal?

I've got no self-interest in this at all. Although if you want a couple of shares in a cotton wool concern, I can help you there.

Right. It's good to see you.

(Pulls out paper from suit pocket.) 'No child will live in poverty…' God, I haven't worn this jacket for ages.

No, it's been a while, hasn't it?

It's very good to see you. I'll think up another crazy idea and come back, Bryan.

I look forward to it.

THE HON. NICK MINCHIN, MINISTER FOR FINANCE AND ADMINISTRATION

In which the three-card trick is explained

Senator Minchin, thanks for your time.

It's very good to be with you, Bryan, and thank you.

You seem very keen to push very hard for this abolition of compulsory voting?

I am very keen on it personally, Bryan, but can I point out that we're not going to do it.

That is the view of the government, is it?

Yes. This is not our policy as a government and it's not going to be introduced. We're not going to do it.

Have you had a compulsory vote on this issue?

In the Cabinet? No. That's not the way we reach our deliberations in the Cabinet.

OK, how do you do it?

Well, normally someone goes out and flies a kite and talks a policy up for a month or so and the prime minister says that he's not sure that is the correct policy.

Then you go ahead and do it and after a while he says that it was his idea in the first place.

No. Not in every case, Bryan. That's not always the case…

It was with the GST.

Yes, but it's not what we did in the case of Telstra, for example. We said, 'We're looking at all the options.'

And then you did it anyway.

No, not initially. We waited.

You did it a bit at a time.

Then we did it in bits, yes.

Just in case it worked.

We had to box a bit clever in that instance. It was a well-known fact the vast majority of Australians were devoutly opposed to our doing it at all.

You fixed them up well and good.

Yes, we had to, but the point I'm making is that in this case what I'm saying about compulsory voting is not government policy and the PM doesn't agree with me.

So how's it going to work?

Just in case it does happen?

Yes. On the off-chance.

Well, just in case it does happen, Bryan, the central idea here is choice. We want to offer people choice. Democracy is all about choice. Democracy means choice.

Does it?

Yes, you choose who you're going to vote for, Bryan.

Weather permitting.

Yes, if you want a vote, stick an application in, we'll have a look at it.

Yes. And you want it to be voluntary?

I do—you don't have to wear a green hat, Bryan, why should you have to vote?

Just because it's a democracy.

Yes. Let's not get carried away. Let's not go nuts.

Should it be compulsory to register a motor vehicle?

Well, yes, I think there's a clear safety issue there.

Compulsory for a driver, say, to have a licence?

Yes. I think there's an important insurance issue there.

Compulsory to pay tax?

Yes. There's parliamentary super, Bryan; where the hell's it going to come from?

So Senator, how's it going to work?

Well, we're not going to introduce it, Bryan.

No, no, no, I understand.

It's not going to happen.

My point is, when you do introduce it, how's it going to work?

OK. Labor voters, for example, why should they be forced to vote?

Don't we need an opposition?

Well, they voted last time and we haven't got an opposition, Bryan.

Have a look at your argument.

That's true.

It doesn't stack up terribly well. Greens are another example. Greens agree about a lot of things. They speak as one. I reckon, if you've got a household full of them, that should count as one vote. One vote per house.

It's not going to happen anyway.

It's not going to happen anyway. But I tell you what—we'd go through those clowns on day one if it did.

Senator Minchin, thank you very much for your time.

Women, there's another idea. Can I borrow your pencil? This is good, keep them coming. Women…

THE HON. PHILIP RUDDOCK, ATTORNEY GENERAL

In which our admiration is given full rein

Mr Ruddock, thanks for your time.
Words, Bryan, cannot express the joy I experience whenever I move among you.

You've taken some flack over this decision to bring in the terrorism legislation on Melbourne Cup Day?
Bryan, the Parliament is sitting on Melbourne Cup Day. It cannot be a surprise that it will be engaging in governmental business while it is sitting.

Yes. I think the criticism is that the government appears to be trying to hurry through contentious legislation while the media and the Australian public's attention is elsewhere.
I understand the nature of that criticism.

What is your reaction to that criticism, Mr Ruddock?
I don't agree with that criticism. I simply make the point, Bryan, that the Parliament is sitting on Tuesday.

And then the next day the IR legislation's coming in?
You bet it is, Bryan.

You don't think there's anything wrong with this?
There is nothing the matter with this whatever, no. These laws, which are new, are not a secret.

Well, no. What went wrong there?
The bastard who is the Chief Minister in the ACT put the bloody thing up on his website.

And you weren't very pleased with that?
I cannot tell you, Bryan, how pissed off I was that a person elected to public office in this country would willingly divulge what we were going to do to the public.

Is that not the democratic way, though?
It is a constitutional crisis of exactly the kind you describe, yes.

Well, Mr Ruddock, what can you do about it?

We will be taking advice on this issue, as we do on many issues, Bryan.

What advice will you be taking?

We will be taking advice of the kind we took when we put all those asylum seekers in prison.

Why did you take legal advice in that instance?

Because the Constitution, Bryan, provides that only judges may imprison people.

What did that advice say, Mr Ruddock?

I cannot reveal to you the precise nature of the advice.

What did you do as a result of that advice?

I got myself another portfolio.

No, I meant what did the government do?

The government argued that it was not putting people in prison.

What was the government doing?

The government argued—successfully I might say—that it was putting people in *administrative detention*.

What's the difference?

Administrative detention, Bryan, is two words.

Those problems are now over, aren't they?

They are not over, no. The Immigration Minister spends an enormous amount of time and many millions of dollars dealing with problems devolving from those issues.

What are those problems?

Problems relating to the appalling treatment of those people.

Which people?

The persons who were seeking asylum in this country.

When?

During the time they were in prison.

Mr Ruddock, thanks for your time. Have a great Cup day.

My Cup day, Bryan, will be significantly better than yours or my name's not Rumpelstiltskin.

THE HON. KIM BEAZLEY, LEADER OF THE OPPOSITION

In which things are going exactly according to lack of plan

Mr Beazley, thanks for your time.
Very good to be with you, Bryan, and good evening.

Mr Beazley, Mr Howard's popularity has declined significantly.
I'm not surprised, Bryan. They've got this IR legislation which is a dead-set shocker and they've smeared it all over the media at a cost of $20 million. I'm not surprised.

But why hasn't your popularity gone up? There are only two of you and his has gone down. Why hasn't yours gone up?
Yes, you would think so. What do the figures say? Who's the preferred prime minister?

Makybe Diva.
That's a horse isn't it? Who's second?

iPods.
I give up. Who's next?

Couple number four in 'Dancing With the Stars'.
Well, am I there at all, Bryan?

Yes. You're equal fifth.
Who with?

Missy Higgins.
Bryan, it's no secret we've been pinned down by some pretty accurate enemy fire this year. We have to…

Mark Latham is technically on your side, isn't he?
Yes, he is, but you don't expect a catherine-wheel to go off up your jacksie every morning, Bryan. We've struggled. Be honest.

Yes, but you're with the government on the terrorist legislation.
Oh, yes, we are. That's very important.

Because Mr Howard showed you something nasty in the woodshed?
Bryan, Mr Howard has had a frank briefing with me describing in detail whatever it is.

Can you tell me what it is?

No, I can't. That would be very irresponsible of me. But I think it speaks very well of John Howard that he would take a bipartisan approach on an issue of this importance.

And did Mr Howard tell you why we are a terrorist target?

Not in detail, no. But he did say it had absolutely nothing to do with our support for the war in Iraq.

How does he know that?

George Bush told him.

We're a bit tight for time tonight. I was just wondering if you could go through this list here and tell me if there's anything in here that you disagree with.

This is a list of government policies.

Yes. Just have a browse. See if there's anything you don't support?

Anything I don't agree with?

Yes, and then we'll discuss it.

I don't see anything immediately.

Voluntary student unions?

No, we're with the government there. We want the student amenities in the universities to be paid for of course…

And how will they be paid for?

No idea.

Strong position.

(Reading.) This all looks good to me, Bryan. Immigration, Aboriginal health, defence…

Foreign affairs?

Foreign affairs, yes. Aged care. Why do you want me to find fault with this? Are you trying to get me in trouble with the prime minister?

Mr Beazley, you are the leader of the opposition.

Leadership is the key concept there, though, isn't it, Bryan?

Rather than 'opposition'?

Well it's not the job of an opposition simply to oppose.

Mr Beazley, if it's not their job to oppose, what *is* the job of an opposition?

Bryan, the point I'm making is what this country needs is *leadership*.

How would you know?

A bloke told me in the lift.

So there's nothing in this list that you disagree with?

I don't know that we'd be entirely happy about this environment thing here, for example.

OK. How would you improve their policy on the environment?

I don't think we'd change the policy. We might structure the department differently. I don't like the look of the car park, for a kick-off.

Stay with the fossil fuels?

Oh, yes. The four-wheel-drives are good for business. Good for all Australians.

Yes, good. OK, Mr Beazley, thank you very much.

Always good to see you, Bryan.

Could we send in the next applicant, thanks?

Next applicant for what? Next applicant?

(Phone rings.) **Thanks, Mr Beazley. Hello, yes? Pardon? There's a horse in reception?**

THE HON. KEVIN ANDREWS, MINISTER FOR EMPLOYMENT AND WORKPLACE RELATIONS

In which Sisyphus leans into his work

Mr Andrews, thanks for your time.

Good to be with you, Bryan. Good evening.

You've dismissed huge demonstrations this week against your IR legislation.

Yes, they were fairly predictable. We thought that'd probably happen.

Will they have any effect?

No, of course they won't. Ninety-five per cent of people went to work.

So we won't be doing any AIDS research in this country?

No AIDS research? Why not? I don't see…

Well 95 per cent of Australians don't have AIDS.

Bryan, my point is that the unions are an archaic, smokestack organisation. It's not surprising to me that their mode of expression is basically irrelevant.

What should they have done?

A touch of the forelock wouldn't have hurt, I'd have thought.

Mr Andrews, there's a fair old alliance against you in this. It's not just the trade unions, is it?

Bryan, can I have a private word with you? You've got a bit of a problem here. I saw you involved in these protests. You marched in the street the other day…

Like a lot of Australians who have concerns about what you're trying to do here.

Well, you're biased aren't you, Bryan? I'd rather talk to someone who's not biased on this issue.

So would I.

I am not biased. You think I'm biased?

Of course you're biased.

We're not biased. We're the government. We're the government of the country.

Of course you're biased. You're bringing in this legislation.

I wasn't running about in the bloody street the other day, protesting against what's going on in this country.

Yes, which also concerns me. You think this is all right.

Bryan, I know it's all right. We've shown it to the Business Council. They reckon it's an absolute cracker.

Why don't the churches think it's a good idea?

Because they're biased.

Why don't the social welfare bodies think it's a great idea?

Because they're biased. Why do you think employer organisations and the Business Council reckon it's such a pearler?

They're biased.

Oh don't be ridiculous, Bryan, they're the people who understand the economy best.

Mr Andrews, would you agree that the government's IR reforms take power away from the employees and give it to management?

That's a very broad generalisation.

It may well be, but is it true?

As it happens it is true but it's a very broad generalisation and I want you to understand its broadness.

Will there be a Fair Pay Commission for executives?

No, that's not what the Fair Pay Commission is, Bryan, it's not for executives. Why do you ask?

Because if people see executives paying themselves these obscene amounts of money and workers are having their conditions taken away from them...

...they might get biased, yes.

They might get very biased indeed, Mr Andrews.

It's a fair point, Bryan.

Will you do something about that?

We might have to do something about that.

What will you do?

Keep executive packages out of the paper for a fortnight until we've got away with it.

It's a pity Telstra announced they were firing 12,000 people this week, wasn't it?

Yes, the timing wasn't terribly good, Bryan. Of course there's nothing the government can do. The government doesn't own Telstra.

And whose decision was that?

Bryan, I'm happy to talk about IR reform, but I'd rather talk to someone who isn't biased, do you understand that?

Exactly my position. Couldn't agree more. Thanks for joining us. You're fired.

THE HON. PETER COSTELLO, TREASURER OF AUSTRALIA

In which our donors are criticised for their donations and our appointments are criticised for being appointed. For goodness sake

Mr Costello, thanks for your time.

Nice to be with you, Bryan, good evening.

You're under some pressure over this appointment to the Reserve Bank board, aren't you?

No, I'm not at all.

Oh c'mon, Mr Costello.

I'm not under any pressure. Bryan, let me clear about this. This is a media beat-up. Mr Gerard has been on that board for two and a half years and he's been a very, very good, valuable member of the board.

Yes, but, Mr Costello, there are questions about this, aren't there? Whether he should have been appointed to the board in the first place?

There always will be questions about an appointment of this kind, Bryan. It's a political appointment.

Mr Costello, I wasn't going to question Mr Gerard's performance on the board.

Well, that's good, Bryan, because he's raised the tone of the bloody joint as far as I can see.

Yes, but the questions don't relate to his performance, do they, Mr Costello? They relate to his appointment.

Well, let's have that discussion by all means. I'll be open about this, Bryan, it is rumoured, it is said that Mr Gerard donated over $1 million to the Liberal Party.

Yes, $1.2 million.

Yes, and it is said, Bryan, that he got the appointment on the basis of having done that.

Is that true?

Haven't finished, Bryan. It is also and further said, Bryan, that Mr

Gerard was in dispute with the Australian Taxation Office.

Yes, one of the biggest disputes they've ever had.

And it is said, Bryan, that that dispute is now resolved.

Is it said how it was resolved?

It is said that he gave them $150 million.

Yes, he did give them $150 million.

Oh, he did, did he? How do you know that?

They announced it, that's how the matter was settled. That's public knowledge, Mr Costello.

I'm the Australian federal treasurer, Bryan, it would be inappropriate for me to know that.

Mr Costello, what was the dispute about?

The dispute was about some money, Bryan, that had gone away on a kind of holiday.

Kind of holiday? Where did it go?

Well, it was on a kind of...gap year.

Schoolies?

Schoolies, yes. But the matter is resolved now, Bryan, but the point I want to make is that it wasn't Mr Gerard who had a dispute with the ATO.

That's right. It was his *company*.

It was his *company*, yes.

Yes, I understand that.

Mr Gerard's name is 'Mr Gerard'.

Yes, Robert Gerard.

His company is 'Gerard Industries'.

Completely different.

Completely different, Bryan, totally different.

Has there ever been an instance of a person benefiting from something done by a company that he was a director of?

Well, we Googled that, he and I Googled that before I put him on the board of the RBA. We sat there and we Googled it together.

Did you type his name in that little box?

We typed his name in the little box, yes.

And then hit 'search'?

No, we hit 'I'm feeling lucky'.

And what did it say?

It said, 'Congratulations, you are now a member of the Board of the RBA'.

Thanks for your time, Mr Costello.

Bryan, if you don't like these things, you know, you want to lift your game. Go online and see how to apply yourself, then go to the website.

What, to the RBA website?

No, the Liberal Party website, Bryan. Replay the interview, you'll see how it works.

BLEAK HOUSE

2006

THE HON. JOHN HOWARD, PRIME MINISTER OF AUSTRALIA

In which we have a play with the remote

Mr Howard, thanks for your time.

It's good to talk to you, Bryan.

Are you excited about the Commonwealth Games?

Yes indeed. Very impressive. I think all Australians love sport. It's the thing that unites us as a nation of knockabout white sport-loving Australian blokes. Or 'families' as I like to call them.

It's a great thing for Australia.

It is. I've sent my congratulations to the bloke who runs Victoria.

Steve Bracks.

Ron Walker. I think he's done an excellent job.

Mr Howard, I wonder if I could ask about the new media ownership proposals in Australia?

Yes, Bryan. As I understand it, there'll be a shotgun start so I suggest people get there early. Seating isn't allocated so…

When will this be?

Well they're already running the heats I think, now. There's been some activity already.

Whereabouts?

In the stock market.

There has been some criticism that the new regime protects the players who currently dominate the market.

Only in the sense that they can buy other media in the same market.

Won't that mean a *lessening* of diversity?

No, because foreign owners can now buy into the Australian market.

Foreign owners like who?

News Limited is a foreign company. Can West.

Aren't they already here? News Limited own 70 per cent of the country's newspapers.

That's right.

This is under the foreign ownership restrictions.

Yes, and those restrictions will go.

Isn't Channel 10 owned by a Canadian company?

It is. But under the current restrictions they're prevented from owning more than all of it.

Those restrictions will come off?

Those shackles and fetters will be removed, Bryan, and…

Open slather.

If you've spoken to Helen Coonan directly there's very little I can add.

No, I haven't. Mr Howard, in the discussion of your protection of local content in television…

Yes, important point; local programming will be very important and must be safeguarded.

In rural and regional Australia.

Yes. They want to see their own news. They want to see news from their own area.

Yes, why is the discussion always about news?

Because people want to see their own news. And so they should. They live in that region and they want to see the stories that are happening there.

My question though, is why is news the only category mentioned?

It isn't. I just talked about *regional* news. But there's sports news, shopping news…

What about other programs made here in Australia?

Like what?

Documentaries. History programs.

There'll be no law preventing those things from happening.

Who'll pay for them?

If there's a market for those things there'll be people who'll stump up the money.

The market won't be determined by the audience though. It'll be determined by the owners. What about Australian drama?

Australian drama?

Yes.

No. You've got a bit over-excited there, Bryan. I suggest you have a glass of water or something.

Thank you, Mr Howard.

A few deep breaths.

(Bryan looks into the camera.) **We invited the leader of the opposition to participate in this discussion, but unfortunately he was available.**

THE HON. KIM BEAZLEY, LEADER OF THE OPPOSITION

In which we are drawn back to the classics

Very good to see you, Bryan, how have you been?

Good, thanks, very good. Big week for you?

Huge week for everybody. Where do you want to start, Bryan?

In what regard?

Well, you know, do you want to ask me any questions? There's been a fair bit going on. Julia Gillard's gone off like a catherine wheel.

Yes, I read about that.

Still that's probably an issue for Stephen Conroy, really.

He's running the party, after all, isn't he?

There's a lot going on. The government's obviously known what AWB was doing from the kick-off.

Who knew?

Bryan, we've got the biggest deficit in our history. We'll be selling uranium in a minute.

I know that, yes.

I don't want to worry you but I've got a few things I could say about this.

Have you?

Yes.

Oh really? What?

Well could I preface my remarks by saying broadly speaking on the big issues, I think the government's doing not a bad job.

Yes, I read that in the paper, you saying that.

Well, I could enlarge on that, Bryan.

Well, I'm sure you could Mr Beazley, I'm sure you could.

Bryan, what are you reading?

A thing about Nero.

Nero. Who's Nero?

He was high up in the Roman Empire.

Oh, yeah. What did he do?

It's quite good. What did he do? He fiddled while Rome burnt.

What do you mean 'he fiddled'?

He played the fiddle, apparently.

Oh, he was a musician.

Yeah, but I don't know whether he was all that talented, really.

Well, he must have had some talent.

I think the point of the book is, Mr Beazley, that Rome was burning.

The whole joint was on fire?

Yes.

And what did he do?

Well, Nero could have done something to stop it burning but he didn't. He played the fiddle instead and still the place burnt down.

He must have had a talent though, Bryan. Not everyone can play the fiddle. I take my hat off to him.

No, I don't think he was particularly talented.

Well, what's the title of the book?

Fiddling While Rome Burns.

Fiddling, Bryan—

You're actually missing the point about this, though.

I think I've got the point.

Do you? What do you think the point is? The point is Rome burnt while he was fiddling and he could have done something about it.

No, no, good on you, Bryan, good on you. *(Giving up and going back to his own reading.)*

Incidentally, what are *you* reading?

I'm just reading one of those how-to books.

Oh really What about?

I'm thinking of taking up a musical instrument.

Really, which one?

The triangle Bryan. 'Ding' it says here. Make a note of that, will you?

THE HON. JOHN HOWARD, PRIME MINISTER OF AUSTRALIA

In which new management techniques are formalised

Mr Howard, thanks for your time.

Pleasure, Bryan. Good to see you and thanks for inviting me on the program. *(An anthem begins. Mr Howard stands.)*

What's that?

The national anthem, Bryan. I think we should stand.

Why is the national anthem playing?

Because Australia is doing so well. It's a terrifically successful country.

Mr Howard, it's hard to have a serious conversation while all this is going on.

You'll get used to it, Bryan. It's not everyone's cup of tea but it's the way we do things at the moment and it seems to work well.

It's a bit distracting this, isn't it? How do you concentrate?

I am concentrating.

Don't you find it a distraction?

I find it rather relaxing. People love it.

How are we supposed to have a sensible discussion about anything?

Normal business goes on all the time. I make announcements about government policy all the time.

That's what concerns me. They used to interrupt a Cabinet meeting if Australia won the Ashes. Now you don't interrupt sport to have a discussion about government policy.

Yes we do, Bryan.

No you don't, you announced your new IR legislation during the Melbourne Cup.

Yes, but we didn't bring it in until the Commonwealth Games.

Were you at the closing ceremony?

Yes, it was magnificent.

What did you especially like about it?

It kept the uranium deal we've done with the Chinese out of the papers.

And you've decided to restructure the board of the ABC?

Yes, we did that during the swimming.

Can I ask you about this cyclone that went through Queensland?

Larry.

Yes, why did it happen?

I don't know. It's weather isn't it, cyclones?

Have we signed the Kyoto Protocol yet?

I don't know. I'd have to check.

Who would you check with? You're the prime minister.

I'd need to check with the minister for selling coal.

Can you just sign this, please?

What is it?

It's an acknowledgment that we had this conversation, that I asked you about environmental damage and cyclones.

Why do you want a signed document?

We don't want the government to say it wasn't told about the connection between global warming and weather change.

Why would the government deny it had been told something?

Do you know anything about how the international wheat trade works?

No, but I could ask Alexander Downer.

Why ask Alexander Downer?

He won't know either. He's very reliable. Wave to that bloke.

Who is he?

John So. He's famous. Hello John.

What are you going to do when this music finishes?

They'll start the Anzac Day music any minute.

THE HON. ALEXANDER DOWNER, MINISTER FOR FOREIGN AFFAIRS

In which the 'It wasn't me, sir' argument is given a run at the national level

Mr Downer, thanks for your time.
Pleasure.

Congratulations on the sale of uranium to China.
Thank you. This is a very important development for Australia. To be part of the great boom in the Chinese economy.

It must be very complicated, the international uranium market.
It is. It has been very complex. Perhaps especially at the diplomatic level.

So you understand it?
The international uranium trade?

Yes.
Yes. We do. We couldn't have done this were that not the case.

So the Australian government must be very good at it indeed?
Yes, I think we can take some pride in our understanding of the international uranium trade.

And yet you don't understand the international wheat trade.
No. Bryan. That's not at a fair point. The government does understand, in broad outline, the scope and nature of the international wheat trade.

But no one told you anything about how it actually happens.
That was the difficulty, yes.

You weren't told things?
We had no idea what was going on.

So what haven't you been told about the uranium trade?
We don't know that yet.

When will you know what you haven't been told?
We don't know that either.

What for example, is a peaceful purpose?
A peaceful purpose is an aim which is not bellicose.

It's a long way away?

No, it's not warlike. It's not to be used in weapons.

Because that's what the uranium we're selling to China will be used for, isn't it?

Peaceful purposes, yes. That's been made very clear.

Can peaceful purposes be imposed on another nation?

No, that would be a contradiction in terms.

Isn't that's what's happening in Iraq?

No that's Freedom and Democracy.

So you *can* impose freedom and democracy on another country?

Well no, I think scientific tests have so far proven that you can't.

I thought it was mission accomplished two years ago.

Yes. It turns out, however, that the idea of an Iraqi is slightly problematic. There are three ethnic groups who live in the area we call Iraq.

Nobody told you?

Again, Bryan, my office wasn't informed.

Will we be selling uranium to India?

I don't know yet.

You haven't been informed?

Nobody's said a dickiebird.

Thanks.

(*He dials a number on his mobile phone.*) Helen Coonan, please. Helen? I've got one for you. Bryan Dawe.

THE HON. JOHN HOWARD, PRIME MINISTER OF AUSTRALIA

In which the headmaster feels he must take action

Sit down, John. What a mess.

What's wrong?

You know very well what's wrong, John.

I haven't done anything wrong.

Do you know a boy called Saddam?

No.

He says you do. He says you attacked him.

That wasn't me. That was George.

Saddam says you were there too.

I wasn't.

George says you were there too.

Yes I was. George and I beat him up.

Why did you beat him up?

Because he had a brain exploder.

What's a brain exploder?

It's a thing that explodes brains.

How do you know he had one?

George told me.

How did George know?

Someone leaked the information to George.

Who leaked the information to George?

George did.

Did Saddam really have a brain exploder?

No.

Is there such a thing?

Yes.

How do you know?

George has got one. I've seen it.

I think we might have to separate you and George. Saddam says

you sold him some food.

While we were attacking him?

Yes.

That doesn't make sense.

None of this makes sense, John. Saddam says he was your main buyer.

Saddam is a crook.

How do you know that?

We had to bribe him to get him to buy the food.

Do you know a boy called Vaile?

No.

Mark Vaile?

What class is he in?

He's repeating year 7.

Why?

He can't keep repeating year 6.

Why doesn't he leave and get a job?

He wouldn't be any good. He can't remember anything.

I think he's a mate of Downer.

No, he's not a mate of Downer.

How do you know?

Trust me. Do you know a boy called Cole?

Yes, Coley, he's a good guy.

Yes, you were on camp with him?

Yes. Good bloke.

Do you know the AWB building down the street?

Yes.

Have you and Cole been writing on it with spray cans?

No.

Don't you and Cole go past it every day?

Yes, but we've never done anything to it.

John, it's got bottoms all over it.

Bottoms?

Someone's sprayed big nude bottoms and other toilet drawings all over it.

We didn't do that.

Is this yours? Did you write this?

What is it? 'Terms of Reference'. No.

Is that your name at the bottom? Read the name.

John Howard.

Keep reading.

'Good on you Coley. We'll get a couple more spray cans after school.'

Right. Now get out. I'm sick of this whole thing. Send Peter in, will you?

THE HON. NICK MINCHIN, MINISTER FOR FINANCE AND ADMINISTRATION

In which the enlistment program hits a few small hurdles

Nick Minchin, thanks for your time.
Pleasure.

You've decided to sell Medibank Private.
That's right, Bryan. The government shouldn't be in the medical insurance business.

What business should the government be in?
I don't know that the government should be in business at all.

So you're selling out?
Yes, we're giving Australians an opportunity to purchase a stake in their known future.

Like you did with AWB and Telstra.
Exactly.

Will it be as successful as what's happened to AWB and Telstra?
We hope it will be even more successful.

Telstra has been a real triumph for government policy, hasn't it?
To a degree it has, Bryan, although there might be one or two better examples.

Didn't Telstra offer Australians a chance to purchase a stake in their own future?
It did, Bryan. I don't think there's any question that ideologically it was the right thing to do.

And who did they purchase their shares in Telstra from?
From themselves. It was publicly owned.

So no brokerage?
No, plenty of brokerage, Bryan, that's where the money is in these things.

Did a lot of people buy Telstra stock?

Yes, Bryan, sadly it was one of the most successful floats in the history of the equities market.

What went wrong with Telstra?

It's easy to be wise afterwards.

There must be reasons it went so badly.

They were landed in wrong place.

The first wave or the second wave?

Both, but the third wave didn't get out of the boats.

I had a brother in the third wave.

The Queen's Own T3s.

Yes.

Was he all right?

He's still there. We send him socks and stuff.

We're sending in support. They've done a fantastic job those people but they'll be pulled out of the line and…

You're sending in replacements?

Yes.

Who are they?

Privates.

Yes, but what regiment?

Medibank.

Medibank Privates.

Yes, they'll go well up there.

Is Tony Abbott going?

Tony and I would love to go but someone's got to stay here and plan the attack.

Attack on who?

Tony and I haven't even met yet. We'll make an announcement.

When the time comes.

Yes, cough will you. Very good.

THE HON. KIM BEAZLEY, LEADER OF THE OPPOSITION

In which it is seen that there is a reason for everything

Mr Beazley, thanks for your time.

Pleasure. Good to be here.

Yes. *(Bryan relaxes. He smiles at his guests.)*

Would you like to ask me some questions?

No thanks. Just happy to have you here.

Why am I here if you don't want to ask me anything?

We need balance.

Balance?

Yes, balance in the program.

Balance.

The ABC is very concerned with balance.

What is balance?

I've got no idea. It's not a decision I make. It's upstairs.

Balance with what?

We've had the prime minister in a couple of times. We need to balance that out.

With me.

Yes.

How do I balance the prime minister?

You're still with the Labor Party?

Yes, I'm the leader of the Labor Party.

Yes. Even better.

So what do we do?

Doesn't much matter. How's the economy?

Hard to say.

The war in Iraq?

Very difficult to say. Not really our war.

Health? Education? IR? The environment? What are you doing?

I thought I might try to finish the crossword.

That's 'apathy'.

What is?

That one ending with a y.

Which one?

Six-letter word meaning 'laziness or want of energy'.

No, I've got that one.

What is it?

'Policy'.

Policy?

Apathy? Could be. So what's this one down here?

What is it?

He was *blank* to be elected into high office for a decade.

How many letters?

Ten.

Triumphant.

Oh.

What did you have?

Wilderness.

No, it ends in a t.

Why?

Because that one across is Green voters.

'A generation of disaffected young people'?

Yes. What have you got?

Bugger them.

That doesn't fit.

It does if you colour a couple of these other squares in black.

What's that big one running down the side?

'Reason given for the war in Iraq'.

Thanks for coming in.

Doesn't fit.

No, I'm thanking you.

Oh. Have you got a rubber?

A MINING ENGINEER

In which we appreciate the importance of physics

Thanks for coming in.

Good evening, Bryan.

You must be happy this great drama is over.

Fantastic achievement by everyone involved.

Yes. Can you describe the actual engineering problem?

Yes, the ground level is here and the…

I've seen the diagrams in the paper.

Yes, they show it pretty well.

It is amazing. Take us through it. How did it start?

Originally there was a sort of collapse.

In the ALP?

Yes, in the main shaft.

The polls had given way.

Yes. But we got some thermal-imaging equipment and it showed that there was some life down there.

This is underneath?

Yes, a long way down.

This was Bill Shorten.

Yes, but he was a long way down and he was a trapped under very heavy rock.

But he was OK?

Yes he seemed to be.

What had happened?

A large Beazley had become dislodged and had fallen into the shaft.

Above him.

Yes, and there was no way that was coming out.

It couldn't be winched to the surface?

No, it was wedged.

Too heavy?

And everything underneath it was trapped.

Could you drill through the Beazley?

We could but we had to be very careful.

You didn't want to get into worse trouble.

No, and then the Beazley turned out to be a lot thicker and harder than we thought.

Five times the density of concrete, I was told.

Yes. Belt it with a crowbar it doesn't even leave a mark.

Hence the delay.

Yes, which is why it took us so long.

How was Bill going through all this?

Remarkable. The resilience of the guy.

How did he keep his spirits up?

We were getting messages to him through a tube.

How was he?

He was good. He knows all the words to 'My Way'.

And then he walked out?

He walked out, waving.

Will the mine be closed?

That's a decision that'll be made over ensuing days.

Have the TV networks talked to Bill Shorten? This is an amazing story.

It is. It's astonishing. I imagine Bill is talking to the networks.

What will those discussions be about?

I don't know.

But Bill knows all the words to 'My Way'?

He does, and he'll bring his own lights.

THE HON. BRENDAN NELSON, MINISTER FOR DEFENCE

In which we thrill to further good news from Ordnance

Brendan Nelson, thanks for your time.

Pleasure.

Can you explain this business with the Seasprite helicopters?

Yes. Do you know what a helicopter is?

Yes. It flies vertically.

No, this is a Seasprite.

Has a propeller up here.

Correct, but they don't fly.

I thought a helicopter was a kind of plane.

This is a Seasprite. You want to talk about helicopters? Or the ones we've got?

The ones we bought. Didn't we buy a billion dollars worth of helicopters?

No, we didn't.

It says here we paid a billion dollars for Seasprite helicopters.

That's right, we did. You might have confused what we paid for them with their actual value.

They're not worth a billion dollars?

Can I just point out I wasn't working here when this purchase went through.

Did these helicopters cost us a billion dollars?

They did.

And why aren't they worth a billion dollars?

Well, they might be. I don't know what they're worth. Metal prices have gone though the roof.

Metal prices.

Yes, we might get a few bob for them. Demand from China and India.

What's the matter with these helicopters?

Nothing the matter with them. Provided you don't try to fly them they're probably as safe as a church.

Are they new?

No, they're secondhand. But they were a very good buy. Only driven to the shops and things.

Little jobs.

Yes, little jobs. On a Sunday.

Where did we get them?

We got them on ebay I think.

What are they for?

They're part of our defence capability.

On the ground.

As it happens, yes, they patrol the hangar they're kept in.

They keep that hangar safe.

Yes, you'd have to be a fool to go in there.

Why?

Why would you want a helicopter that doesn't fly?

So they're useless?

No, they're not useless.

They're just not helicopters.

That's right.

But we might find another use for them?

We'll have to.

What?

You know when you're reading the paper on a windy day and the pages keep blowing away?

Hold them down with a helicopter?

Chopper them down, yes.

Thanks for your time.

Have you got a boat?

Yes.

You'll need a mooring.

A Seasprite?

Extra reliability with a Seasprite.

Thanks for your time.

Buy one, get one free. Call now.

THE HON. KIM BEAZLEY, LEADER OF THE OPPOSITION

In which we get the tractor out of the river again

Mr Beazley, thanks for your time.

Pleasure.

You've made a bit of a stand on the matter of the AWAs.

Yes, this is pretty important stuff. This IR legislation is no good and we're going to fix it.

What are you going to do?

We're going to tear it up and make any existing AWAs null and void.

Rollback.

No it's not rollback. It's a response to this medieval legislation. We're going to fix it.

So how will you do it?

When we get into power, we will introduce legislation…

This is based on your being elected to government?

Yes, once we are elected, a Beazley Labor government will introduce legislation that will…

Mr Beazley, is there anything you can do without getting elected into government?

You need to be elected into government to change the laws of the country.

OK. I see.

You understand that, don't you?

Yes, sort of. So people would need to vote for you to make this happen?

Yes, that's the idea.

Well, just explain that to me.

That's pretty basic. In the democratic system we have here, if you're not happy with the government, you have a choice.

This is in Australia?

Yes, this is the model I'm describing.

This is now?

Yes, of course it's now. This is the current situation I'm describing.

So just using your argument, if you're living in Australia and you don't like the policies of the government, what do you do?

You vote for the opposition.

Yes, this is federally?

Yes. There are two main parties with a realistic chance of forming a government. You don't like the policies of one of them, you vote for the other one.

And their policies would be different.

Yes, that's the choice.

Say on asylum seekers.

Well, on most issues.

Let's say you weren't happy about the war in Iraq.

Well, that's a difficult one. As I say, Bryan, on most issues.

Or women's rights.

Women's rights?

Or the environment.

Let's take another issue, Bryan. Let's take these AWAs.

OK. If you were opposed to the IR legislation...

Yes, then you'd vote for us.

Because your policies are different from the government's?

Yes, there's a clear choice.

Well good luck, Mr Beazley. I hope it goes well for you.

Thanks, Bryan. Is that it? How do we get out of here?

There's a choice. You can go out here or over there.

What's the difference?

There's no difference. Just a choice.

MR ANDREWS,
A CONCERNED PARENT

In which it is sometimes necessary to have a word with the parents

Mr Andrews, come in.
Thanks.
Please. Take a seat.
Is it about Kevin?
Yes.
I got your message. Is everything OK?
Well, we've just done a big project review. Are you aware of what Kevin was doing?
Well we knew he was working on something. There's a lot of clutter in the house.
It's to prepare them for the sort of task they might be asked to conduct as adults.
Yes, we understand that. It's great training. I don't know about Kevin's project in detail but I actually printed a lot of it out at a work.
OK, well just to put you in the picture, Kevin's taken on industrial reform.
Industrial reform?
You seem surprised.
Yes, don't know why he chose that. What would Kevin know about industrial reform?
I was going to ask you about that.
How did he go?
Well, I think he did a lot of work.
Yes, he did.
Look, to be honest he's got into trouble in couple of key areas. Have a look.
(He reads.) Mmmm. Who are these companies?
They're all companies who don't wish to be associated with Kevin's project.

I'm not surprised. They're dependent on their staff, a lot of these companies. They'll go broke if they introduce...

I'm sure he thought he was helping them.

He hasn't thought this through though, has he? Did you talk to him about this? Has he had help with this?

Yes, I've spent a lot of time with Kevin.

Did he know these companies didn't want a bar of it?

Yes. He said that proved how good the proposal was.

Because these companies wouldn't wear it?

Yes.

Oh dear. *(He reads on.)* Oh God, and he's made it compulsory to dock your own workers' pay if they go to a meeting about it.

Yes, he's actually put them in a difficult position.

Couldn't the staff just say they're not coming in because they got pissed watching the soccer or they've got a pretend cold? Nobody would mind if they didn't come to work.

No, he's painted himself into a bit of corner.

It's all a bit of a mess, isn't it?

Imagine if this were happening in real life.

It'd be hopeless.

Can I ask you something? Is he happy, do you think? Kevin? Is he a happy kid?

I'd describe Kevin as a very normal kid.

Does he have any friends?

He doesn't relax easily socially, I have to say.

Has he ever mentioned John or Philip?

Yes. And Nick, he's got a friend called Nick.

Yes. Is he easily influenced?

This is not the Kevin we know. Is there something we can do at home?

He obviously thinks he's done pretty well with this project.

I think he thinks it's a triumph.

He might need some counselling.

Yes. I might take him camping for a couple of days. Get him out of the house.

Yes, move him round a bit.

Quite a lot I think. I might take the dog. *(He looks again at his son's work.)* Poor bugger. He tried so hard.

THE HON. JOHN HOWARD, PRIME MINISTER OF AUSTRALIA

In which we search for balance

Thanks for coming in, Mr Howard.

Pleasure to be here, Bryan.

Quite a week.

Yes, it has had its moments.

Yes.

Is that what you want to talk about?

Yes, we'll go in a minute. *(Bryan is looking off camera.)* **I just want to get some comments from the public if I can.**

Comments?

Yes. We're just ringing around now. The switchboard is trying to find someone.

OK.

We just thought it would be a good idea to get some views from the public.

About this week and all this Costello stuff?

Well, about Mr Costello's allegation…

…that I'm a liar?

Yes.

That's not the way I would characterise those events.

No, of course it's not, Mr Howard.

As a matter of interest Costello has been asked many times over the years whether we had a deal over the leadership.

I know. I've asked him myself.

And he said no.

He said absolutely not.

So who is he calling a liar?

Well yes, you've both got arguments that don't work.

So what sort of response are you trying to get from the public?

We want to get someone who's surprised. Just to provide a context.

Surprised about what? Surprised that Peter's been telling porkies?

Surprised that you're both now saying publicly that you can't be trusted.

Where are you looking?

We've done New South Wales, Queensland and Victoria. South Australia and Western Australia.

Where are you now then?

Lord Howe Island. Nothing?

Try Christmas Island.

Christmas Island's not part of Australia any more.

(Remembers.) That's right. We even lie about where the country finishes.

It would be good if we got someone who is surprised, just for contrast.

Have you tried Alan Jones?

The board won't wear him.

How very surprising. Actually, why would people be surprised? They keep voting me into power.

That's right.

I told them I wasn't going to bring in a GST, there were people throwing their babies in the sea, they should buy Telstra stock, WMDs…

That's true. We're not going to find anyone. We'll go without them.

OK.

Are you ready?

Yes.

Mr Howard, are you a liar?

That's not a word I would use.

Thank you.

Good to see you, Bryan. Good on you.

A VOTER

In which the customer is under some pressure to be right

Thanks for your time.

Thanks for inviting me in.

I wonder if I can just go through some your responses to these questions.

Yes, which ones?

You're a voter?

Yes.

Where are you?

We're in Mortgage Vistas.

OK.

Up the Gearing Highway.

Whereabouts?

It's about an hour and a bit up there. You know where the Kiddies are?

Yes.

Through there and it's about another 2.5 per cent.

Near Dreamy Peaks.

Yes, you've gone a bit far there. It's between Dreamy Peaks and Bigborrowings.

What's that river up there?

The Barrel.

Yes, that's beautiful.

Gorgeous. Take a camera if you go up there. You look directly down the Barrel from Bigborrowings.

Yes. It's lovely country up there.

It's a wonderful place to bring up petrol prices.

Children.

You're telling me.

OK, and you were polled recently?

No, I think that's just these new trousers.

I mean you've been questioned by pollsters.

Yes, sorry, that's correct.

And you've said you believe Peter Costello's version of the meeting with John Howard.

Yes. *(Off.)* Interest rates haven't gone up have they? Still 8 per cent?

But you don't want Peter Costello as prime minister.

That's right. *(Off.)* Let me know if they go up. They're still 8 per cent?

And you've put Kim Beazley ahead of John Howard as preferred prime minister.

Yes, that's right.

So if there was an election you'd vote for Kim Beazley.

No we wouldn't. John Howard's the prime minister. *(Off.)* Interest rates? Still 8 per cent?

So why have you said you'd vote for Kim Beazley?

John Howard's got to know this IR stuff stinks. We're not having that. That's terrible. That's not the way we treat each other in Australia.

Have you said that anywhere here?

Yes.

Where?

We said if there was an election tomorrow we'd vote for Kim Beazley.

What'll you do if interest rates go to 10 per cent?

They're not going to do that are they?

I don't know. Nobody can control interest rates.

Give us a ring if interest rates go to 10 per cent.

And what'll you do?

I'll tell you what I really think of John Howard.

THE HON. PHILLIP RUDDOCK, ATTORNEY GENERAL OF AUSTRALIA

In which an obsession with fairness and reason is successfully held at bay

Mr Ruddock, thanks for your time.
Hang on. Not quite ready. I'll be with you in a moment. Can you get me a glass of water please?

Mr Ruddock, I'd like to talk to you about the case of Mr David Hicks.
I'm just waiting for a glass of water.

Mr Ruddock.
Yes, I'll be with you as soon as I can.

David Hicks has now been in jail for four and half years. Mr Ruddock.
I'll be with you as soon as I get a glass of water.

Are you thirsty?
The question is not whether or not I am thirsty now, Bryan. The point at issue is whether or not I might become thirsty at some future time.

How long do you think it'll take you to get David Hicks out of Guantanamo Bay?
(Water arrives.) Thank you.

Are you ready Mr Ruddock?
Yes.

Mr Ruddock, thanks for your time.
I am attempting to contain my excitement, Bryan, at the prospect of discourse with you on what I genuinely hope will be a range of issues.

Mr Ruddock, when will the Australian government bring David Hicks home?
I have asked the United States government to expedite the matter of Mr Hicks and I have received assurances from them that the matter will receive their urgent attention.

When will the matter receive their attention?
The matter, Bryan, will receive their *urgent* attention.

When will the matter receive their urgent attention?

At some future time. I have received those assurances and I expect them to be fulfilled.

Fully.

The concept 'fully' inheres in the doctrine of Fulfilment.

And they'll do this urgently?

Those are the assurances I have received.

When?

At some future time.

You've said you are opposed to the nomination of David Hicks' father, Terry Hicks, as Australian Father of the Year.

What I have said is the nomination of Mr Hicks for Father of the Year is a politicisation of the award.

But giving it to Mr Howard was not?

The award, when conferred on John Howard, was a monument of objectivity and a model of its kind.

Nothing political about it?

No, Mr Howard was given the award as a private citizen.

Where did they send the award?

To Kirribilli House, Bryan. That's where he lives.

So a political figure is someone whose son has been locked in a foreign jail for four and half years without any charges being laid against him?

That is my understanding.

Have a glass of water, Mr Ruddock.

The issue is not whether I should have a glass of water now…

…But whether you should have a glass of water at some future time.

Have a good weekend, Mr Ruddock.

Thank you, I will, Bryan.

What will you be doing?

Swimming, Bryan.

THE HON. PETER COSTELLO, TREASURER OF AUSTRALIA

In which a key contender is reeled back in by the peloton

Sit down, Peter. This is a bit unusual. You want to pull out of the bike club?

Yes, I'm sick of it.

I thought you were dead keen.

I was.

I thought that's why you came here.

It was.

You told me you were the hope of the side.

Yes I was.

'Bikes R Us' you told me.

That's right.

So why pull out?

We haven't got a bike.

What happened to the bike?

It got nicked.

We've got a bike, Peter. I've seen it out the window here, being ridden around.

It's gone.

Where has it gone?

Someone borrowed it and never gave it back.

Do you know who's got it?

No.

Did you ask around?

Yes.

What did people say?

They told me to shut my face and go back to class.

OK, so you want to pull out of the bike club.

Yes.

But you want to remain vice-captain of the bike club.

Yes.

Why do you want to be the vice-captain of a club you want to pull out of?

I want to have a go on the bike at some point.

But the bike's gone, hasn't it?

Yes, the little bugger.

You can't have a bike club without a bike, Pete.

The club still needs office-bearers.

To do what? You haven't got a bike.

Admin and stuff.

Admin? What sort of thing?

Bike maintenance.

Whoever's nicked the bike will be maintaining it, surely?

There's still stuff to record.

Like what?

The number of wheels.

There'd be two, wouldn't there?

Should be. There used to be, yes.

It's a bicycle. It's a two-wheeler.

Yes, but we have to be sure.

Won't you get bored?

There's nothing else to do.

What about developing some other interests?

I hate interests. I'm sick of interests.

What about learning something about politics?

Like what?

Do you know what's happening in Lebanon?

Snotty Downer was talking about Lebanon.

Yes. What was Snotty Downer saying about Lebanon?

Nothing.

How could he be talking about Lebanon without saying anything?

He reckons it's not easy but he's being doing it for a fortnight.

That must require a lot of skill.

He reckons he has to be very careful.

Why?

In case he says something.

THE HON. JOHN HOWARD, PRIME MINISTER OF AUSTRALIA

In which the party of business demonstrates a safe pair of hands

Mr Howard, thanks for your time.
Pleasure.

Can you explain what's happening at the moment with Telstra?
Yes, a decision will be made about whether to sell the rest of Telstra or whether to pop it into the future fund.

When will you make that decision?
We'll be doing that last week.

You'll be making that decision last week?
That's right.

Why didn't you announce it last week?
Because the bloke who runs the future fund doesn't want us tipping landfill into his boatshed; he's told us to clear off.

Why doesn't he want it?
He reckons he's trying to run a successful investment fund. You can see his point.

Why wouldn't you sell it to the market?
Because the price has fallen and we can't get what we want for it.

It was Australia's biggest company at one stage, wasn't it?
Yes, that's right, it was. We fixed that.

What about all the people who bought stock in it?
Yes, people should be very careful with investments of course. Investment decisions need to be very carefully planned.

Weren't they buying, as you yourself said at the time, 'a stake in Australia's future'?
Yes, Bryan, I'm afraid it's beginning to look as if that might have been exactly what they were doing. My heart goes out to them.

Have you thought of ebay?
Sell Telstra on ebay?

Why not? It's an international market. A bloke sold an apostrophe on

it the other day for $6.50.

I wouldn't know how to do it.

I'll do it. It's easy *(He gets his laptop and sets to the task.)* **What will we call it?**

'Highly successful international telco.'

No, ebay's an honour system. You have to describe the item accurately.

OK. 'Pile of old tat, mostly post-war.'

What about, 'Ex-government equipment. Give-away prices.'?

Good. Go with that.

OK. 'Seller's name.' What do you want to call yourself? Give yourself a name.

'Not my fault.'

Already taken.

Really? Someone's already called himself 'Not my fault'?

Yes. A bookseller. Someone trying to sell some books.

What books?

Three titles: '*I Am Responsible for Interest Rates, Vote for Me and Get a House*', '*Petrol Prices Might Go down Again*' and '*Iraq for Beginners*'.

Good luck getting rid of that stuff.

Who do you want to be?

I'll be 'Selling off the Farm'.

OK. *(Types.)* **Selling-off-the-Farm. Do you want to set a reserve?**

Yes let's set a reserve price.

Yes, we can't afford to just give it away.

Exactly it's a major public institution. We've got to be responsible. I'm the prime minister.

What'll I put?

One hundred dollars

I'll put $101.

Yes, then we might get 100 net. Cover our costs. Good thinking, Bryan.

'Do you wish to attach a photo of the item?'

Hell no. We want to sell it.

'Photo unavailable.'

Do you want to put: 'Hurry, hurry, be in early for this, can't last'?

No. You did that the first time.

Yes, that's possibly where we went wrong.

Oh! What's this! There's a bid!

Good. Where from?

Three Mexicans and Mrs Alston.

Sell it!

Done. Gone!

What did we get for it?

One dollar fifty.

Well done.

See, it's easy. What else have you got?

(*Off.*) Barry! What else have we got?

THE HON. KIM BEAZLEY, LEADER OF THE OPPOSITION.

In which we are united in our admiration for one of the great talents

Mr Beazley, thanks for your time.
Very good to be with you, Bryan.

How are things going?
Very well thanks.

Are you busy?
I have been busy.

You're on the road a lot, aren't you?
I am. I've been in Sydney, Brisbane, Melbourne, Canberra.

And are you getting a good response?
By and large, yes. There are critics of course. Not everyone likes it.

They'll always be critics, I suppose.
Exactly. But generally I think things are good.

You're getting good notices in the press.
Yes. You need plenty of coverage. You can build from there.

It's quite an achievement. How do you do it—the John Howard impression? Because you don't look like very like him.
No, but I've lost some weight and the John Howard impression's not the only thing I do.

I know but that's what you're best known for. How do you think your way into the character?
I've looked at John Howard for a long time. I studied the way he talks, the sort of things he says, the way he stands.

What sort of thing does he say?
He has quite conservative views. He's all for big business. He's a nationalist; he's very big on the army.

Yes, you've caught all those things perfectly.
He's very keen on the popular media; he's on talkback all the time.

Just like you. It really is uncanny.
He gets photographed a lot at sports events.

Yes, he's got that Australian tracksuit.

Yes, the one under his suit?

Yes.

Yes I've got one on order. He's got a right-wing position on social issues like race and gender, sexuality.

You've got those pretty well now too.

I think the key is to keep expressing a concern for Australian families.

Yes, it's a great smokescreen, isn't it?

It's brilliant. No one knows what it means and I tell you what, when you do it, you can hear a pin drop.

I bet you can. You do it very well. You're very good at that. Have you ever met him, the real John Howard?

Yes, we bump into each other from time to time.

Does he like what you do?

He loves it.

He's a fan?

I saw him this week, Monday I think it was. It was in Adelaide.

What did he say?

He'd seen the thing I'd done on uranium.

Was he nice about it?

He said even he couldn't tell the difference.

High praise. That's great!

He actually congratulated me on it publicly, on Tuesday.

He did. You must be chuffed.

It doesn't get any better than 'I congratulate Mr Beazley on his courageous stand on the question of uranium'.

Mr Howard, thanks for your time.

Ha ha ha ha. Got you there, Bryan.

God he's good.

THE HON. NICK MINCHIN, MINISTER FOR FINANCE AND ADMINISTRATION

In which the sales department hits its monthly target

Senator Minchin, thanks for your time.
Very good to see you, Bryan. How's the family? Are they well? The family?

My family? They're good thanks.
That's the way. Lovely weather. Did you get out today, did you, Bryan? Beautiful day Today, wasn't it?

Yes. I wouldn't mind some rain.
My word. Rain would be good. My word. Couldn't we all do with some rain? That'd be just the ticket, some rain.

Nice to see you again.
Yes, just thought I'd pop back, Bryan. I was in the area. I've got something here that might interest you. I can get you in on the ground floor. I know one or two people involved in this, through Rotary. I can look after you, although we'll need to get the paperwork done today.

No thanks. I don't want any T3 stock.
No I heard you on that one. This is not T3. This is a different product; a product that might just be perfect for you. It's catered more to your needs.

What is it?
It's in the health area. Always a winner, the health area. A great sector to be in. You ever seen a poor doctor?

No, look, I don't think so thanks.
It's not for you, Bryan. You can put this in the bottom drawer for the kids. It's an investment in the future.

What is it?
Medibank Private. It's rock solid. It's a health insurance business. Government guaranteed.

It's government guaranteed?

It will be until you buy it, Bryan. You'll be on your own a bit then, but it's beautifully set up.

No, I don't want to buy a health insurance business.

It's walking out the door Bryan. Listen, that's it now. *(He cups his ear.)* You can hear it. That's it, walking out the door.

What does it do?

It insures people against the costs involved in healthcare.

Do people need health insurance?

Yes. Health costs are rising all the time.

Why are health costs rising?

Because of the cost of medical insurance.

Insurance costs are driven by insurance costs?

That's it Bryan, it's a perpetual motion machine; you can't lose. I'll give you my card.

Sales manager?

Yes.

I've had a couple of your other operatives in here this week. Who's John Howard?

Head of Marketing. He's overall strategy.

Who's Peter Costello?

Young fellow, yes. Group accountant.

What's the price of Telstra stock?

Don't know Bryan. Not a stock we cover. This is the one for you. It's got hot and cold folding doors. It's whiff-waffed on both sides and bevelled all around. Two kinds of water, clean and dirty. Guaranteed not to rip, tear or bust and it comes with batteries and a leather case. Bryan, if I had the money, I'd be buying this one myself.

(Not buying it.) **Thanks for coming in.**

(Giving up on Bryan and looking elsewhere.) Waste of time. Hello. What's your name? Floor manager. Good on you, Floor. Is there a Mrs Manager?

THE HON. JOHN HOWARD, PRIME MINISTER OF AUSTRALIA

In which it is clear that John may have to repeat a year

John, sit down. This exam you've done.

How did I go?

I think there's some work to do before the end of the year.

How did I go in economics? I bet I aced that.

I'm talking about economics. You didn't sit any of the other subjects did you?

I had a virus.

Why didn't you sit geography?

I couldn't find it.

You got lost?

No. I didn't. It did.

It's a shame you didn't do the history paper. Most of the questions were on parts of the course we've covered.

Like what?

'The similarities between Vietnam and Iraq.'

There aren't any.

That's right. We covered that. You would have got that right. 'If you invade a country and create a power vacuum, what is the next phase of that country's history?'

Peace and democracy.

See? You'd have romped it in. 'Those who do not study the mistakes of history are doomed to...' What?

Only get back into office if there's no opposition.

Yes, it's a shame you didn't get there. Now, this economics paper...this is a bit of a worry.

Why?

Question 2. 'Who is responsible for interest rates?' You've written 'The prime minister if they're low...'

Yes.

...'The bogeyman if they're high.'

Yes.

Who's the bogeyman?

He's a really frightening kind of interest rate spook.

An interest rate spook who puts up interests rates?

Yes, after prime ministers have got them down.

There isn't a bogeyman, John. Interest rates are set by central banks, largely as a function of international trade balances.

Prime ministers can sometimes keep them low.

Prime ministers can't control interest rates at all and everyone knows it. You'd be laughed out of court if you said this in public. Question 7. 'If oil prices doubled what should the government do with the fuel excise?'

Yes, I didn't know that one.

You've written 'develop a car that runs on onions'.

Yes.

Did you think of 'lower petrol excise'?

(*Quietly.*) Bugger it.

Question 9. 'Why can't Australian families afford housing when debt is at record highs?' You've written 'there's not enough land'.

Yes.

There's not enough land? John, you haven't given this much thought have you. Did you read the question properly?

Yes.

Question 12. 'Why would a country invest its entire savings pool in the domestic housing market?'

Yes, what did I put?

You put, 'Who cares about industry? Vote for me.'

I had a virus.

Why have you pinned a cheque to your exam paper?

That's not a cheque. It's a first homebuyer's grant.

How are they going to buy a house now interest rates are going up and petrol prices have doubled?

They can't.

Why not?

There's not enough land.

(*Off.*) Get matron will you, quickly? Just stay where you are, John. Help is on its way. Not enough land. Have you ever been in a plane?

Yes. There's nothing down there.